STRANGE BUT TRUE

UFOs

STRANGE BUT TRUE

UFOs

ROWAN WILSON

Sterling Publishing Co., Inc.
New York

Library of Congress
Cataloging-in-Publication Data Available

10 9 8 7 6 5 4 3 2 1

Published in the United States and Canada in 1997 by
Sterling Publishing Company, Inc
387 Park Avenue South, New York, NY 10016–8810

Originally published in Great Britain in 1997. Produced by Magpie Books,
an imprint of Robinson Publishing Ltd.

Illustrations courtesy of Popperfoto

Distributed in Canada by Sterling Publishing
c/o Canadian Manda Group, One Atlantic Avenue, Suite 105
Toronto, Ontario, Canada M6K 3E7

ISBN 0–8069–0577–8

Printed and bound in the E.C.

Contents

1

Fire from the gods

On a February morning, in the 22nd year of the reign of Pharaoh Thutmose III, a circle of fire appeared in the sky over Egypt. It hung silent and motionless, and brought with it a foul smell. The Pharaoh was informed and he meditated for a while on what should be done. While he thought, more circles appeared, filling the sky completely. They shone with a brightness that hid the sun. Then, in the hour after dinner, the circles moved off towards the south and disappeared from view.

This is the first recorded UFO sighting in human history. It dates from around 1500 BC. In their broadest definition, unidentified flying objects have always been with us.

The UFO phenomenon, as most people understand the term, started in the late 1940s, with large waves of sightings first in the US and then across the globe. Before that, no real attempt to collect and collate reports of UFOs had been tried. In light of the interest that has arisen in the last half of the twentieth century, many researchers have looked back into the history books to find evidence.

Many "Ufologists" would argue that UFOs show that we are not the only intelligent life in the universe. That is a very modern conclusion to draw. In the past, UFOs have been interpreted as signs from the gods, or even as the gods themselves. Where we see them in recorded history, they are described in ways that made sense to the people of the time. On September 24, 1235, the army of General Yoritsume was preparing to camp for the night in the Japanese countryside. Suddenly, there was some commotion towards the southwest of the camp and soon the whole army could see why. Tiny lights were dancing in the sky, circling each other like insects. The weird display continued throughout the night, fading only with the coming of morning. General Yoritsume, like any good military man, immediately demanded an explanation. He set his wise men the task of explaining the lights. They undertook what was probably the first scientific investigation of a UFO sighting. They puzzled at the problem and studied the evidence until they hit upon an answer. They reported back to the General. The lights, they said, were caused by the wind fluttering the stars.

In their zeal to find evidence of UFOs in writings from the past, many Ufologists have pointed to incidents in the Bible that might qualify. For example, the Prophet Elijah was said never to have physically died. He was "translated," that is to say, taken directly to heaven from earth without dying first. The means of his "translation" was a fiery chariot that carried him up to God. In light of modern cases where people claim to have been abducted by UFOs, some researchers have argued that Elijah's "translation" was a UFO abduction. According to them, the Old Testament's writers just described the event by applying their own system of beliefs. A full list of "UFOs" in the Bible would fill this

Dr J. Allen Hynek was the first to produce a classification system for UFO sightings. First he divided them into two categories based on how far away the object was – *Distant Encounter* (for objects over 500 feet away) and *Close Encounter* (for those nearer). The first category he divided into the fairly self-explanatory sub-categories of *Nocturnal lights*, *Daylight discs* and *Radar visuals*. *Close Encounters* had their own sub-divisions:

Close Encounters of the First Kind. These take place when a UFO is seen close by, but does not in any way affect its surroundings.

Close Encounters of the Second Kind occur when the UFO actually affects something, such as burning the ground beneath it or frightening animals.

Close Encounters of the Third Kind were the last of Hynek's categories. In these, the occupants of the UFO are seen directly by the witnesses.

As claims of UFO abduction have become more and more common, the definition of the last category has been stretched to include boarding an alien vessel, and intelligent communication with its occupants. However, some purists object to this drift in meaning and use two new categories *Close Encounters of the Fourth* and *Fifth Kind* to describe these new cases.

book on its own. In the Old Testament, the pillar of smoke and fire that led the Jews in the wilderness could be a UFO. In the New Testament, the star that led the Magi to the manger could have been a UFO. There is just too much material to work on, and with little

3

agreement among scholars as to which Biblical events are historical and which are just metaphorical, the task of identifying genuine UFOs in the Bible is virtually impossible.

A similar problem crops up with the UFOs that were seen by Alexander the Great. In 329 BC, as they swept across Asia and the Middle East, Alexander and his army were crossing the river Jaxartes. As they approached the Indian shore of the river, two "silver shields" appeared in the air and dived toward them. The horses shied and the men broke rank and ran. The shields appeared again in 322 BC. This time it was during the battle of Tyre, in what is now Lebanon. As Alexander's army battered at the city's walls, a large silver shield with four smaller companions dived out of the sky onto Tyre. They fired beams of light that blew holes on the wall and toppled towers. Alexander took full advantage of the phenomenon and his troops rushed into the city.

Unfortunately, this incredible sighting (straight from the pages of *Amazing Stories*), may be just a metaphor. Alexander was believed by many ancient writers to be the Greek god Dionysus, reborn as a human being in order to conquer the world. Naturally, a god would summon supernatural forces to fight in his battles. It is possible that the writer created the incidents to reinforce the legend and to express Alexander's divinity.

Roman writers also recorded UFO sightings. The historian, Julius Obsequens, writing in the fifth century AD, described objects that resembled "ships in the sky" appearing over Italy in 216 AD. He also records lights in the sky over Rome in 203 AD and 90 BC.

Pliny The Elder, in his *Historia Naturalis*, describes a UFO seen in 66 BC as a spark from a star. The light fell to earth, where it grew to the apparent size of the moon. Then, as quickly as it had fallen, it flew back into the air. He also describes an object that was seen during the consulship of Lucius Valerius and Gaius Marius. At sunset one evening, a "burning shield" appeared in the sky over Rome. Sparks shot from its edges as it crossed the sky from east to west.

Pliny gives us the name that Romans used to describe the phenomenon – "night suns." To have a name for them, it is reasonable to assume that the Romans saw them quite often. Of course, Roman observers would probably have described shooting stars and other normal phenomena as "night suns." On the other hand, shooting stars do not fly back into the sky like Pliny's "spark from a star" . . . .

Pharaoh Thutmose's circles of fire, and General Yoritsume's dancing lights, both remind us of modern "flying saucer" sightings. Not all ancient UFOs are as easy to reinterpret.

In the Irish borough of Cloera, during a Sunday Mass in 1211 AD (at the church of St Kinarus), an anchor attached to a rope fell from the sky. The rope stretched taut straight up into the heavens and it dragged the anchor for a second, whereupon it caught firmly in the arched doorway of the church. A crowd gathered to watch the marvel and peering up to see where the rope was attached, just made out the hull of a ship, high in the sky. The anchor was plainly stuck and soon the spectators saw a speck leave the ship and float its way down. As it approached, they saw that it was a man making motions like a swimmer diving down into the water. When the man was close enough to see the gathered crowd, he panicked and headed back to the

5

vessel. Shortly afterwards, the anchor-rope was cut and the ship sailed away. The anchor was put on display in the church.

This sighting seems, on the face of it, to be a tall tale dreamt up to impress tourists. However, it is strangely similar to a wave of unidentified airship sightings that swept Texas and Arkansas in 1897. The newspapers of the time carry many reports of a weird dirigible, with external wheels and strange mechanisms, being spotted by many groups of witnesses. Some even reported that it produced orchestral music. A Mr John Barclay told the *Houston Post* that he had been woken by his dogs late one April night. Having read of the airship sightings, he got out his gun and went to investigate. Sure enough, in the sky over his house hovered a strange black shape with lights attached shining downwards. The lights seemed brighter than normal electrical illumination. While Mr Barclay stood amazed, a man approached him out of the darkness. Superficially there was nothing strange about him.

The man asked Barclay to lower his gun, and then gave him a ten dollar bill and asked him to fetch some objects in exchange. He wanted some lubricating oil, two cold chisels, and some bluestone. Barclay did as he was told and soon returned with all but the bluestone, which he had been unable to find. Having no change, Barclay offered the man his ten dollar bill back. He refused it.

The man thanked Barclay and told him not to follow him. As he was going, Barclay finally thought to ask the man who he was and where he was going. The man replied that he could not tell him who he was, but that they were going to Greece and should be there in two days time. Having said that he walked off into the night. Almost immediately, the craft flew off "like a shot out of a gun." The *Houston Post*'s report ends by stressing that Mr Barclay was an honest and reliable witness.

Four days later, the airship was seen above Merkel, Texas, this time dragging an anchor along the ground. Like the Cloera flying ship, this vessel's anchor soon snagged on an obstacle, in this case the railway tracks. Some people returning from church saw the rope and, looking up into the night sky, saw a black shape with bright lights attached, much like Mr Barclay's unknown visitor. After a few moments, a small man shinned down the rope. He was wearing a light blue sailor suit. On catching sight of the crowd that he had attracted, the man cut the rope and the ship sailed off to the north-east.

> For the year 732, the *Anglo-Saxon Chronicle* records the following, "In this year terrible portents appeared in Northumbria, and miserably afflicted the inhabitants; these were exceptional flashes of lightning, and fiery dragons were seen flying through the air."

All the above sightings, with the possible exception of Pharaoh Thutmose's circle of fire, sound nothing like our modern idea of a UFO. In 1878, in a sleepy regional newspaper called the *Dennison Daily News* of Texas, the first of the new breed was reported:

Mr John Martin, a farmer .... had his attention directed to a dark object high in the northern sky. The peculiar shape and velocity with which the object

7

seemed to approach, riveted his attention, and he strained his eyes .... when he first noticed it it appeared to be about the size of an orange, after which it continued to grow in size. After gazing at it for some time, Mr Martin became blind from looking and left off viewing to rest his eyes. On resuming his view, the object was almost overhead and had increased considerably in size and appeared to be going through space at a wonderful speed. When directly over him, the object was the size of a large saucer and .... at a great height.

Here the word "saucer" is used for the first time, and since he'd hurt his eyes, we can also assume that – in spite of its first dark appearance – it shone in a manner typical of modern UFOs.

One of the first writers to make a habit of noting down reports of "unknown objects seen in the skies," was Charles Fort. Born in Albany, N.Y. in 1874, he made a poor living as a journalist for most of his life. In revolt against his bad tempered father, he spent his life finding reasons for undermining authority.

In 1916, when he was 42, a small legacy enabled him to spend his days in the New York Public Library, searching periodicals for accounts of strange and unexplained events. His four books – beginning with *The Book of the Damned* (1919) – should have made him famous and rich, since his fellow Americans have an unquenchable appetite for strange stories and extraordinary theories. Unfortunately, Fort was short on theory – his method was simply to take any odd events he could find and throw them higgledy-piggledy into books that had no particular direction or argument. Fort simply had no gift of story telling, with the consequence that, when he died in 1932, he was virtually as unknown as when he had started.

But his miscellaneous collections of "damned" (by damned he meant excluded by science) facts are like old attics full of rubbish through which other collectors can rummage for hours – provided they can stand the dust.

Among Fort's typical observations are the following: "Maunder was at the Royal Observatory, Greenwich, November 17, 1882, at night . . . . In the midst of the Aurora a great circular disc of greenish light appeared and moved smoothly across the sky . . . . the thing passed above the moon, and was, by other observers, described as 'cigar-shaped' 'like a torpedo,' 'a spindle,' 'a shuttle.'"

This seems to be the first recording of the typical "cigar-shaped," UFO that has been reported so frequently.

Here is another: "I was standing on the corner of Church and College Street . . . . when, without the slightest indication or warning, we were startled by what sounded like a most unusual and terrific explosion . . . . raising my eyes, and looking eastward along College, I observed a torpedo-shaped body, some 300 feet away, stationary in appearance, and suspended in the air, about 50 feet above the tops of the buildings . . . . This object soon began to move, rather slowly, and disappeared over Dolan Brothers' store, southward. As it moved, the covering seemed to be rupturing in places, and through these the intensely red flames issued."

Fort's biographer, Damon Knight, comments, "The reports of unknown flying objects collected by Fort bear little resemblance, as a rule, to the "flying saucer" stereotype. Some were simply moving lights in the sky, some torpedo-shaped, some triangular. Others were like nothing on Earth, but showed definite evidence of structure. There was a 'thing' seen by the crew of the barque *Lady of the Lake* on March 22, 1870.''

The Tunguska Object

On June 30, 1908, the inhabitants of Nizhne-Karelinsk, a small village in central Siberia, saw a bluish-white streak of fire cut vertically across the sky to the northwest. What began as a bright point of light lengthened over a period of ten minutes until it seemed to split the sky in two. When it reached the ground, it shattered to form a monstrous cloud of black smoke. Seconds later there was a terrific roaring detonation that made the buildings tremble. Assuming that the Day of Judgment had arrived, many of the villagers fell on their knees. The reaction was not entirely absurd – in fact, they had witnessed the greatest natural disaster in the earth's recorded history. If the object that caused what is now known as "the Great Siberian Explosion" had arrived a few hours earlier or later, it might have landed in more heavily populated regions and caused millions of deaths.

As it later turned out, the village of Nizhne-Karelinsk had been over 200 miles away from the "impact point", and yet the explosion had been enough to shake debris from their roofs. A Trans-Siberian express train stopped because the driver was convinced that it was derailed and seismographs in the town of Irkutsk indicated a crash of earthquake proportions. Both the train and the town were over 800 miles from the explosion.

Whatever it was that struck the Tunguska region of the Siberian forestland had exploded with a force never before imagined. Its shockwave travelled around the globe twice before it died out, and its general effect on the weather in the northern hemisphere was far-reaching. During the rest of June, it was quite possible to read the small print in *The Times* at midnight in London. There were photographs of Stockholm taken at 1.00 a.m. by natural light, and a photograph of the Russian town of Navrochat taken at midnight looks like a bright summer afternoon.

For some months, the world was treated to spectacular dawns and sunsets, as impressive as those that had been seen after the great Krakatoa eruption in 1883. From this, as well as the various reports of unusual cloud formations over following months, it is fair to guess that the event had thrown a good deal of dust into the atmosphere (as happens with violent volcanic eruptions and, notably, atomic explosions.)

Perhaps the strangest aspect of the Great Siberian Explosion was that no one paid much attention to it. Reports of the falling object were published in Siberian newspapers but did not spread any further. Meteorologists speculated about the strange weather, but no one came close to guessing its real cause.

It was not until the Great War had been fought, and the Russian Revolution had overthrown the Tsarist regime, that the extraordinary events of that June day finally reached the general public. In 1921, as part of Lenin's general plan to place the USSR at the forefront of world science, the Soviet Academy of Sciences commissioned Leonid Kulik to investigate meteorite falls on Soviet territory. It was Kulik who stumbled upon the few brief reports in ten-year-old Siberian newspapers that finally led him to suspect that something extraordinary had happened in central Siberia in the summer of 1908.

Leonid found the reports confusing and contradictory. None of them seemed to quite agree where the object had exploded. Some even claimed that the "meteor" had later been found. But when his researchers began to collect eyewitness reports of the event, Kulik became convinced that whatever had exploded in the Tunguska forest was certainly not a normal meteorite.

These reports described how the ground had opened up to release a great pillar of fire and smoke which burned brighter than the sun. Distant huts were blown down and reindeer herds scattered. A man ploughing in an open field felt his shirt burning on his back, and others described being badly sunburnt on one side of the face but not the other. Many people claimed to have been made temporarily deaf by the noise, or to have suffered long-term effects of shock. Yet, almost unbelievably, not a single person had been killed or seriously injured. Whatever it was that produced the explosion had landed in one of the few places on earth where its catastrophic effect was minimized. A few hours later and it could have obliterated St Petersburg, London or New York. Even if it had landed in the sea, tidal waves might have destroyed whole coastal regions. That day, the human race had escaped the greatest disaster in its history and had not even been aware of it.

Finally Kulik discovered that a local meteorologist had made an estimate of the point of impact, and in 1927 he was given the necessary backing by the Academy of Sciences to find the point where the "great meteorite" had fallen.

The great Siberian forest is one of the least accessible places on earth. Even today it remains largely unexplored, and there are whole areas that have only ever been surveyed from the air. What settlements there are, can be found along the banks of its mighty rivers, some of them miles in width. The winters are ferociously cold and in the summer the ground becomes boggy and the air is filled with the hum of mosquitoes. Kulik was faced with an almost impossible task – to travel by horse and raft with no idea of exactly where to look or what to look for!

In March 1927, he set off accompanied by two local guides who had witnessed the event, and after many setbacks arrived on the banks of the Mekirta river in April. The Mekirta is the closest river to the impact point, and in 1927 formed a boundary between untouched forest and almost total devastation.

On that first day, Kulik stood on a low hill and surveyed the destruction caused by the Tunguska explosion. For as far as he could see to the north – perhaps a dozen miles – there was not one full-grown tree left standing. Every one had been flattened by the blast and they lay like a slaughtered regiment, all pointing towards him. Yet it was obvious that what he was looking at was only a fraction of the devastation, since all the trees were facing in the same direction as far as the horizon. The blast must have been far greater than even the wildest reports had suggested.

Kulik wanted to explore the devastation but his two guides were terrified and refused to go on. So Kulik was forced to return with them, and it was not until June that he managed to return with two new companions.

The expedition followed the line of broken trees for

several days until they came to a natural amphitheater in the hills, and pitched camp there. They spent the next few days surveying the surrounding area and Kulik reached the conclusion that "the cauldron," as he called it, was the center of the blast. All around, the fallen trees faced away from it and yet, incredibly, some trees actually remained standing although stripped and charred at the very center of the explosion.

The full extent of the desolation was now apparent – from the river to its central point was a distance of 37 miles. So the blast had flattened more than four thousand square miles of forest.

Still working on the supposition that the explosion had been caused by a large meteorite, Kulik began searching the area for its remains. He thought he had achieved his object when he discovered a number of pits filled with water – he naturally assumed that they had been made by fragments of the exploding meteorite. Yet, when the holes were drained, they were found to be empty. One even had a tree-stump at the bottom, proving it had not been made by a blast.

Kulik was to make four expeditions to the area of the explosion, and until his death he remained convinced that it had been caused by an unusually large meteorite. Yet he never found the iron or rock fragments that would provide him with the evidence he needed. In fact, he never succeeded in proving that anything had even struck the ground. There was evidence of two blast waves – the original explosion and the ballistic wave – and even of brief flash fire, but there was no crater.

The new evidence only deepened the riddle. An aerial survey in 1938 showed that only 770 square miles of forest had been flattened, and that at the very point where the crater should have been, the original trees were still standing. That suggested the vagaries of an exploding bomb, rather than that of the impact of a giant meteor – like the one that made the 600 foot deep crater at Winslow Arizona.

Even the way that the object fell to earth was disputed. Over 700 eyewitnesses claimed that it changed course as it fell, saying that it was originally moving towards Lake Baikal before it swerved. Falling heavenly bodies have never been known to do this, nor is it possible to explain how it could have happened in terms of physical dynamics.

Another curious puzzle about the explosion was its effect on the trees and insect life in the blast area. Trees that had survived the explosion had either stopped growing or were shooting up at a greatly accelerated rate. Later studies revealed new species of ants and other insects which are peculiar to the Tunguska blast region.

It was not until some years after Kulik's death in a German prisoner-of-war camp, that scientists began to see similarities between the Tunguska event and another even more catastrophic explosion – the destruction of Hiroshima and Nagasaki with thermonuclear devices.

Our knowledge of the atom bomb enables us to clear up many of the mysteries that baffled Kulik. The reason there was no crater was that the explosion confirmed this – at both Nagasaki and Hiroshima, buildings directly beneath the blast remained standing, because the blast spread sideways. Genetic mutations in the flora and fauna around the Japanese cities are like those witnessed in Siberia, while blisters found on dogs and reindeer in the Tunguska area can now be recognized as radiation burns.

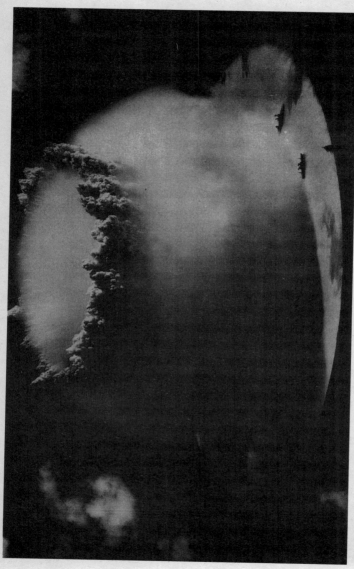

The first "A" bomb explosion at Bikini Atoll, 1946, showing the shock waves travelling sideways

Atomic explosions produce disturbances in the earth's magnetic field and, even today, the area around the Tunguska explosion has been described as "magnetic chaos." It seems clear that an electromagnetic "hurricane" of incredible strength has ruptured the earth's magnetic field in this area.

Eye-witness accounts of the cloud produced by the explosion again support the view that it was some kind of atomic device – it had the typical shape of the atomic "mushroom cloud." Unfortunately, the one conclusive piece of evidence for the "atom bomb" theory is lacking. By the time the area's radiation levels were tested, more than 50 years later, they were normal.

Later investigators also learned that Kulik had been mistaken in his theory about the water-filled holes. They were not caused by meteorite fragments but by winter ice forcing its way to the surface through expansion, then melting in summer. Kulik's immense labours to drain the holes had been a waste of time.

Every year, Russian scientists return to the blast area to search for fragments of the Tunguska object. Every year they admit to finding nothing. Recent American computer simulations have suggested a reason. Planetary scientist Chris Chyba of Princeton and Paul Thomas and Kevin Zahnle of the NASA Ames Research Center in California, modelled what would happen when a large meteor or comet fell through the earth's atmosphere. Their computer simulation revealed that the heat and pressure caused by friction with the earth's atmosphere would flatten the object into a pancake-shaped mass. This mass would collapse almost instantly under the pressure that flattened it in the first place, crumpling it up into a ball again. This process would repeat over and over again within a moment, ripping the object apart to form a cloud of tiny fragments. To an observer on the ground, it would look as if it had been dynamited.

This could explain why the object caused darkness around the world. Instead of having to assume that the debris in the air was thrown up from the impact site, the Ames model predicted that the debris cloud was the object itself, ripped into atoms and spread like a huge cloud over the northern hemisphere.

The NASA computer simulation was also able to calculate the density of the object. Depending upon their density, different objects would tear apart at different altitudes. Using the model, the Chyba team came up with an interesting observation on the popular theory that the Tunguska object was a comet.

Comets are often described as "dirty snowballs." They are chunks of ice laced with rock and dust. An English scientist suggested that a comet was responsible for the Tunguska blast, and the idea has enjoyed a lot of support. The pressure and heat produced by falling through the atmosphere would cause atoms of hydrogen in the comet to fuse and form helium. This would create a nuclear explosion. Although this seemed like a good explanation of the "air blast" seen at Tunguska, skeptics argued that no comet could approach the earth without being seen by astronomers. The only plausible exception to this would be if it was coming from the exact direction of the sun. Chyba's team added another objection. According to their computer model a comet would have detonated far higher in the atmosphere than the altitude of the Tunguska explosion.

Chyba's study seemed to point to a huge meteor, detonating into microscopic debris some miles above

Halley's Comet photographed in 1987 by David F. Malin in
Coonabarabran, Australia

the earth's surface. This conclusion ties in with the fact that earth passes through a cloud of meteors called the BetaTaurids every June and December.

All this seemed to disprove the comet theory. Then, Evans Lyne and Richard Fought of the University of Tennessee at Knoxville and Michael Tauber of Stanford University, examined the Chyba research and noticed a mistake. The Chyba team had assumed that all the pressure and heat generated by friction with the atmosphere would go towards blowing the Tunguska object to pieces. They had forgotten that falling stars shine, and by shining give out some of the heat they are generating in the form of light. Adjusting the computer model to take this into account, Lyne, Fought and Tauber found that the Tunguska object could, after all, have been a comet.

Rather less plausibly, some ufologists have suggested that the Tunguska explosion was caused by a crashing alien spacecraft. One school of thought favors the idea that the ship's nuclear reactors were overheating and that it may have been heading for Lake Baikal to cool them when it exploded. Others note that eye-witnesses observed the object change direction before exploding. This, they say, could have been due to a last minute decision to miss Lake Baikal, in order to avoid setting off a chain-fusion reaction that would have blown the earth in half.

It might be suggested that some of the "scientific" explanations are just as implausible. A. A. Jackson and M. P. Ryan of the University of Texas have suggested that the explosion was caused by a miniature black hole – a kind of whirlpool in space caused by the total collapse of the particles inside the atom. They calculated that their black hole would have passed straight through the earth and come out on the other side, and the Russians were sufficiently impressed by the theory to research local newspapers in Iceland and Newfoundland for June 1908. But there was no sign of the Tunguska-like catastrophe that should have occurred if Jackson and Ryan were correct.

Other American scientists suggested that the explosion was caused by antimatter, a hypothetical type of matter whose particles contain the opposite electric charge to those of normal matter. In contact with normal matter, antimatter would explode and simply disappear. Only atomic radiation would be left behind. But there is even less evidence to support this theory than there is for the black-hole explanation.

Although rarely violent, UFOs can sometimes be devastating. On the night of December 13, 1990, the Soviet radar station at Kuybyshev picked up a large blip approaching them at speed. Two and a half minutes later, the blip broke into many small traces, all maintaining a course that took them to the station. A unit of soldiers was sent to investigate. They saw a large, black, triangular UFO with smooth sides, about 45 feet long. The craft was approaching one of the base's radar masts. As it hovered before it there was a flash and the mast burst into flame. The object stayed hovering in the sky around the base for over 90 minutes, while the mast burned and finally crashed to the ground. Later investigation showed that the steel from which the mast was constructed had completely melted.

Moreover, one Russian scientist has expressed his doubts about whether there ever was a Tunguska object. Andrei Ol'khovatov, a radiophysicist at the Radio

Instrument Industry Research Institute in Moscow, believes that the devastation at Tunguska was caused by an earthquake. He cites recorded cases in which large earthquakes have not only torn up the ground, but also sent tremendous lightning flashes into the air. In fact, several Tunguska eye witnesses described something of the sort, but until now their comments had been discounted.

Ol'khovatov insists that much that went unexplained in the original eye-witness accounts can be explained by his theory. For example, eyewitnesses described three different trajectories for the "meteor," which could be explained as three separate lightning flashes. Objectors point out that the recorded earth tremors at Tunguska were far less violent than earthquake activity in which lightning that might be mistaken for a meteor has been observed. Also, they argue that the circular pattern of fallen trees does not tie in with the earthquake damage.

If Ol'khovatov's theory fails to cover all the reported facts, it is worth bearing in mind that this is also true of every other theory. Despite the recent scientific evidence provided by computer modelling, a complete solution to the mystery of the Tunguska object seems as remote as ever.

2

The Saucer Invasion

In late June 1947, a C46 Transport aircraft disappeared in the area of Mount Rainier, in Washington State, with 32 men on board. A $5,000 reward was offered for anyone who could locate the aircraft. Kenneth Arnold, an Idaho businessman who was also an experienced pilot, decided to try for the prize and took off in his small propeller-driven monoplane on the morning of June 24, 1947, from the airfield at Chehalis to fly across the Cascade Mountains to Yakima, Washington State.

Later that day, he was to describe how, flying at an altitude of about 9,200 feet above the town of Mineral, he was beginning to make a 180 degrees turn when "a tremendously bright flash lit up the surface of my aircraft." A moment later, he saw another flash and saw "far to my left and to the north, a formation of nine very bright objects coming from the vicinity of Mount Baker, flying very close to the mountaintops and travelling at a tremendous speed." Since they were travelling at almost 90 degrees to Arnold's flight path, he was able to calculate this speed at 1,700 m.p.h. Moreover, the craft were not flying in the straight trajectory of a normal aircraft, but bobbing up and down "like speed boats on rough water." "They fluttered and sailed, tipping their wings alternately and emitting very bright blue-white flashes from their surfaces."

Arnold was so intrigued that he decided to land at Yakima and report the sighting. He landed at about 4.00 p.m. and told his story to a manager and discussed it with other pilots, before taking off again for Pendleton, Oregon. By the time he arrived there, he found that the news had preceded him and that among the crowd waiting to receive him was a reporter named Bill Becquette, from the *East Oregonian* newspaper. It was to him that Arnold used the classic phrase that would echo throughout the rest of the century – that the objects moved "like a saucer would if you skipped it across water." So began the mystery of the "flying saucers."

Yet if we look again at the original description of the craft, it is notable that Arnold said "tipping their *wings* alternately" which certainly sounds as if he mistook them for normal aeroplanes.

Arnold's first conclusion is that they were some secret weapon of the United States Air Force, perhaps some type of robot craft, like the German "flying bombs" of the end of the Second World War.

As a result of Becquette's story – which was carried by the Associated Press wire service – Arnold suddenly found himself famous. For three days, he talked endlessly to reporters. It was only when he was back at home in Boise, Idaho, that he was told by the aviation editor of a local newspaper that what he had seen was pretty definitely nothing to do with the Air Force or the United States Government. Later on, Arnold was to come to the odd conclusion that what he had seen was some strange unknown species of animal that inhabit the upper layers of the earth's atmosphere – a theory reminiscent of Conan Doyle's story "The Horror of the Heights."

For some reason, the world was ready for strange stories about Unidentified Flying Objects. The end of the war had seen London attacked by Hitler's V-2 rockets, and after the war, many of the German scientists who worked on the rockets – notably Werner von Braun – were persuaded to go to America to work on the effort to put a man on the moon. Popular magazines were full of articles about space flight, and the possibility of life on other planets. So all over the world, people were ready to take this first sighting of "Flying Saucers" seriously.

What happened next is almost as interesting as Arnold's original sighting. The news literally unleashed a flood of UFO sightings. The first came three days later, when a Washington housewife saw discs "like silver plates" flying over the Cascade Mountains, near where Arnold had spotted them. The following day, June 28, saw three more sightings, one by a pilot over Lake Meade, Nevada, one over Maxwell Air Force Base in Montgomery, Alabama and one at Rockfield, Wisconsin, when a farmer saw some blue, soundless discs flying over his farm. The next few weeks saw dozens more, including no less than 88 sightings on Independence Day, July 4, reported by 400 people in 24 states. On July 7, the first British sighting occurred when a married couple saw "something like a moon, only bigger" fly over the cliffs at Brighton. On the same day, astronomers at Del Salto Observatory, Chile, saw a disc trailing white gases and moving across the horizon at what they estimated at 3,000 m.p.h. On the same day, more UFOs were reported in Italy, Japan and Holland.

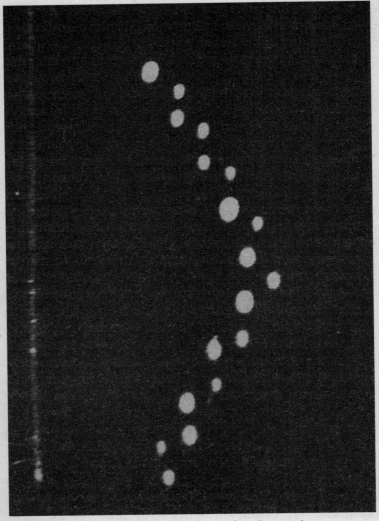

Pictures of the "Lubbock Lights" taken by Carl Hart at
Lubbock, Texas, 1951

Mass hysteria? Some of it certainly was. Yet at least one of the sightings – the one over Maxwell Air Force Base – included a detail that certainly adds to its authenticity. The bright light that zigzagged at high speed made a sharp right angle turn before disappearing.

In fact, this is a highly characteristic observation of the kind that no one would have thought of inventing at the time. But it has been reported again and again in subsequent cases.

The Roswell Incident

During the next ten years there were thousands of sightings – so many that it would be impossible even to mention most of them. But one of the most controversial – the so-called "Roswell incident" – is still hotly debated.

On the night of July 4, 1947, at the beginning of a long Independence Day weekend, two Franciscan nuns, Mother Superior Mary Bernadette and Sister Capistrano were making astronomical observations of the sky above the town of Roswell, New Mexico. Some time just after 11.00 p.m. they saw a brilliant white light plummet to earth. They recorded the event in their logbook.

South of Roswell, 13-year-old William Woody and his father were watching the skies looking for meteors. Around 11.30 p.m., a white object with a fiery red trail crossed their field of vision, heading northwest over Roswell. It did not look like the meteors that they had seen before. It was too bright, so much so that it hurt their eyes. Another thing made them feel this was not the usual shooting star. It was too slow. It fell like a plummeting aircraft . . . .

William "Mac" Brazel worked on the Foster Ranch, north of Roswell. That night he heard a tremendous crash come from out in the fields. It was strange, unlike the thunder that had been rumbling dully through most of the evening. Brazel decided to keep his eyes peeled out when he rode to the ranch the next morning.

What he found was torn metal sheeting and large chunks of debris, which covered a field south of the ranch. All around, the light shiny foil fluttered and glinted in the breeze. The wreckage centred on an arroyo or small cliff and spread across acres of desert scrub. The early morning sun made the whole field shine. Brazel picked up some of the foil. It was indeed as light as it looked. However, when crumpled into a ball, it resolutely unfolded and smoothed itself out. Investigating further, Brazel found that there were many small beams or rods strewn across the field. These were thin and as light as dowling, yet too rigid to break. Try as he might, Brazel could only bend them slightly. When the pressure was released they sprang right back. Intrigued, Brazel tried his knife on the debris – it would not cut. Burning with matches did not even mark it.

Brazel had company that morning – William Proctor, the young son of a neighboring family. The two agreed that they should take some of the material over to the Proctors to get another opinion. Their sheep refused to cross the debris field no matter how much they urged them. So, after a long detour to reach a watering hole, the pair drove to the neighboring ranch with some specimens.

Loretta and Floyd Proctor examined the foil with interest. Floyd tried to cut and burn it (just like Brazel had), with the same lack of success. Brazel suggested that the Proctors drive over and see the field, but they declined – they were too busy. It was a decision they would later regret.

Brazel returned home wondering what to do. The debris was in his way. But he decided to put off the decision until the weekend. He took Sunday afternoon off and drove in to see the Sheriff of Chaves County, George Wilcox, at his office in Roswell.

Covered in dust and wearing scruffy work clothes, Brazel was first seen by a deputy. The rancher explained his problem and brought out a piece of the foil-like debris to show what he was talking about. The deputy had never seen anything like it before. But since it had fallen from the sky, he suggested that it was military business.

Roswell, New Mexico, is surrounded by military bases. They provide jobs and inject money into the local economy. The closest was the Roswell Army Air Field, home of Bomber Squadron 509, the nuclear bomb wing. The B-52, "Enola Gay", that had dropped the H-bomb on Hiroshima was a part of 509 Squadron. Also close by was the army listening post at Alamogordo. Finally, in the desert to the west of Roswell lay White Sands Testing Grounds, the home of US experimental aeronautics. After World War II, the creator of the V2 rocket bomb, Werner von Braun, had been brought to the US to work on secret weapon systems and the newly launched space program. His laboratory was also at White Sands.

At Roswell Army Air Field, Major Jesse A. Marcel was eating lunch when he took the phone call from Sheriff Wilcox. Marcel was the base's Intelligence Officer, which meant that the unidentified debris strewn across the Foster ranch fell within his jurisdiction.

He was intrigued by the description of the wreckage. So, taking a counterintelligence sergeant called Sheridan Cavitt with him, Marcel lost no time in leaving for Roswell. By the time that he arrived it was late afternoon, too late to drive out to the isolated debris field before dark. So Marcel and Cavitt accompanied Brazel back to the Foster ranch house and, as night fell, they examined a large piece of the wreckage that Brazel had dragged back from the field.

It was like nothing Marcel had ever seen. But at least a Geiger counter showed it was not radioactive. Several years earlier, New Mexico had been the site of some of the first nuclear weapons tests.

Early the next morning, Cavitt and Marcel made their way with Brazel out to the crash site. Examining more of the wreckage failed to bring any further enlightenment. Marcel was familiar with most kinds of military hardware, but looking at torn silver shreds clinging to the arroyo, he could not see anything akin to any weapon, rocket or balloon. It was very disturbing.

The metallic beams in the field had a cross section less than a half inch square and were as light as aluminium – yet so strong that, exerting all his strength, Marcel could only bend them slightly. And when he released the pressure, they straightened out immediately. Studying one of the beams closely, he could just make out lines of markings in two colors, like Chinese script. The phrase that kept crossing Marcel's mind was "flying saucer." The local and national news were full of sightings. And here, out in the desert, was mysterious wreckage that defied categorization. Hurriedly, Marcel gathered armfuls of the debris and loaded up his jeep.

Instead of taking it back to Roswell Air Field, Marcel

brought it to his home. He wanted his family to see it. Jesse Jr remembers that morning well. He and his mother were still in bed when Marcel arrived. He quickly roused them and told them to help him carry in the pieces in from the car. They spread the wreckage out on the kitchen floor and began trying to fit it together.

Marcel's wife, Viaud, noticed the strange markings on the beams and pointed them out to Jesse Jr. He later explained that they were leaves, circles and other simple figures. Finally, Marcel packaged up the debris and took it back to the base.

It was the following morning before Colonel William Blanchard, the base CO, examined Marcel's find. He ordered Marcel to take the debris to Fort Worth Army Air Field and show it to General Ramey. About noon that day, Tuesday, July 8, 1947, First Lieutenant Walter Haut (Information Officer for Roswell Army Air Field) composed a press release about Brazel's discovery and distributed it to the local radio stations and newspapers. The afternoon papers received it in time for that day's editions. The *Daily Illni* reported it under the headline "A.P. Wire Burns With 'Captured Disk' Story." The misprints in the article indicate that it had been typeset in a hurry. It read, "Roswell N.M. The army air forces here today announced a flying disc [sic] had been found on a ranch near Roswell and is in army possession.

"The Intelligence office reports that it gained possession of the 'Dis:' [sic] through the cooperation of a Roswell rancher and Sheriff George Wilson [sic] of Roswell.

"The disc landed on a ranch near Roswell sometime last week. Not having phone facilities, the rancher, whose name has not yet been obtained, stored the disc until such time as he was able to contact the Roswell sheriff's office . . . .

". . . . Residents near the ranch on which the disc was found reported seeing a strange blue light several days ago about three o'clock in the morning."

The next morning, most of America was reading about the captured "disc" over breakfast.

Whether all the debris was flown to Fort Worth, or just the part that Marcel recovered, is not known. Sergeant Robert Porter, who flew the B-29 that transported it, later reported that there were four boxes, the largest of which was three feet across and triangular.

Ramey received Marcel in his office, where the debris was already stacked in its boxes. Ramey had been fielding calls from newsmen ever since the Roswell press release and the entire situation was beginning to worry him. After a discussion with Marcel, Ramey decided on a press conference, during which the wreckage would be displayed to the media.

A few hours later, as the assembled journalists contemplated fragments of what was quite obviously a weather balloon, Warrant Officer Irving Newton (a weather officer), assured them – unnecessarily – that the wreckage on the floor of Ramey's office definitely originated on planet Earth. Marcel was present at the conference but kept his silence.

Hughie Green, a Canadian Air Officer (later to become famous as the presenter of the British version of TV talent show "Opportunity Knocks"), recalled how he was driving east across New Mexico on that Independence Day weekend, and how, at first, every local radio station buzzed with the news of the captured alien craft. Then, suddenly, the anticlimactic announcement that the alien spacecraft was just a crashed weather balloon killed speculation stone dead.

The weather balloon story was to remain the accepted view for many years – in fact until 1979, when Major Marcel decided to tell his own version of events at Fort Worth to journalist Bob Pratt.

According to Marcel, what happened was a simple switch. When he had arrived in the General's office that day, Ramey had insisted upon being shown the exact location of the crash site on some charts in another room. By the time they returned to the office, the wreckage that he had carefully ferried all the way from New Mexico had vanished, and in its place, laid out on brown paper, was a torn weather balloon. When Marcel had picked up some of the balloon to examine it, photos had been taken by the base's information officer. Ramey told Marcel that he would attend the press conference and would play along and keep his mouth shut.

Directly after the conference, Marcel said that Ramey had ordered him back to Roswell. Since it was clear that the army had launched a disinformation campaign, Marcel ordered his family to keep quiet about what they had seen that July morning.

Back at Roswell Army Air Field, Marcel found Sergeant Cavitt who had accompanied him on the first visit out to the Foster Ranch. He asked him if he had prepared a report. Cavitt said that he had but could not show it to Marcel, since it was confidential. He added that the order came direct from Washington.

Marcel's first response was irritation since he outranked Cavitt. Eventually, he saw that the Army had the entire situation sewn up. They had used him as a patsy. He was not happy about it – but the opportunity to tell the truth had to wait for 30 years until journalist Bob Pratt came to interview him.

The year following the Pratt interview, Marcel appeared in a TV documentary called "In Search Of," which covered UFO conspiracy theories and alleged crashes. In the film, Marcel repeated his assertion that the debris he had recovered in 1947 was not the remains of a weather balloon, as shown in the official photos. As a result of this new exposure, interest in the Roswell incident flared up again. And as UFO investigators converged on the town and began asking questions, interesting facts began to emerge.

Most of the people who had been living in Roswell at the time of the crash were still around and they, like Marcel, had stories to tell about the days following the discovery on the Foster ranch.

William Woody, the young boy who had seen a slow shooting star on the night of the crash, told how he and his father had decided to go and look for the object they had seen. Early on the morning of July 5, 1947, they had climbed into their pickup truck and driven north on Route 285. As they approached the area where they guessed that the object had landed, they found that every exit east and west off the highway was blocked by military sentries.

Glen Dennis, the proprietor of Ballard Funeral Home in Roswell, told investigators that on the day after the crash, he had received phone calls from the Army Air Field's mortuary officer. The military wanted childsized coffins. Then the officer wanted to know if the coffins he had could be closed to form an airtight seal. As if this was not strange enough, the officer rang back 40 minutes later, to ask about embalming and the effects of embalming fluid on the blood and tissues of a corpse. He seemed to be eager to discover if preserving a body would make it impossible to carry out an accurate medical examination at a later date. Dennis told him that it would and the officer rang off.

Later that day, Dennis told investigators, he had driven out to the Air Field. Ballard's Funeral Home had the army contract to ferry wounded service personnel back to the base and that afternoon, a soldier (who had suffered some minor head injuries, needed Dennis's ambulance service. As they arrived at the base, Dennis saw three army ambulances parked outside the infirmary. Inside two of them, there were torn pieces of metal-like aeroplane wreckage. The third was closed and guarded by a Military Policeman.

As the contracted ambulance driver, Dennis had the run of the hospital's staff areas. Feeling thirsty, he decided to go in for a soft drink. Once inside, he detected that there was something wrong. People were rushing about and shouting. Dennis assumed that there had been a plane crash. A nurse stopped him as he entered the lounge. She was incredulous that he had got into the unit and told him to get out as fast as he could or there would be trouble.

While Dennis tried to explain that he had a right to be there, an officer noticed them and angrily ordered two Military Policeman to escort him out. The officer had heard Dennis mention the crash and before having him ejected, he made a stark threat – "Don't tell anybody you saw anything. Somebody'll be picking your bones out of the sand."

A couple of days later, Dennis contacted the nurse he had met that day and arranged a meeting at the officers' club. When she arrived, she was looking badly shaken, pale and nervous. She told him that the torn pieces of metal he had seen were not from a normal aeroplane. They were sections of a crashed spacecraft. The staff at the hospital had been treating the injured occupants of the craft when Dennis arrived.

On her prescription pad, the nurse drew a picture of one of these "foreign bodies" as she called them. The bodies were humanoid, yet smaller than an average person and slight in build. The only exception to this was the head, which was bulbous and hairless. The creatures had facial features similar to humans. Their mouths were lipless and small, their nose was indented and they had no ears. Their bones, she said, were flexible and tough, like cartilage.

The nurse told Dennis that she had been told to take notes while doctors carried out an autopsy on three of the dead creatures. Two of the bodies were badly mutilated, while one seemed to have survived the crash and only died of exposure once on the ground. The damage to the corpses was such that the doctors suspected that they had been mauled by desert predators. Throughout the examination, an ammonia-like choking smell came from the aliens. Eventually, the autopsies had to be abandoned due to nausea and faintness caused by the gas. The bodies were bagged up and sent down to the morgue.

Dennis's story was precise and detailed. And, of course, quite incredible. Yet many people in Roswell were telling stories that seemed to support it. Frankie Rowe was the daughter of one of Roswell's fire fighters, Dan Dwyer. On July 5, 1947, Frankie remembered, her father had been called out early in the morning. Dwyer told his daughter that they had gone out about 30 miles northwest of Roswell into the desert and there seen "a flying craft" crashed and wrenched to pieces. He said that it looked as if the main pieces of wreckage had already been cleared away before they got there. Dwyer also said that there were bodies at the crash site. Two were dead and bagged when they arrived, but one was alive and seemingly uninjured and capable of walking.

Later, Frankie said, the military had arrived and told them to keep quiet about what they knew of the crash. They had specifically told her, a ten-year-old girl at the time, that if she talked about what she had heard she was liable to get lost in the desert and never come back.

The blockbuster movie *Independence Day*, features a sequence supposed to take place in the top secret underground military facility known as "Area 51." UFO folklore has it that this installation contains all the recovered remains of aliens and their craft that the US government wants to investigate in secret. Although there is absolutely no hard evidence that the base exists, it is known that the US government does have many secret underground facilities.

In 1987, Lloyd A. Duscha, a senior officer in the US Army Engineer Corps, gave a speech entitled, "Underground Facilities for Defence: Experience and Lessons" at a conference on subterranean construction. He spoke for some time about the general theory employed by the army, using as examples well-known nuclear defence installations. He went on, ". . . . there are projects of similar scope, which I cannot identify, but which included multiple chambers of up to fifty feet wide and one hundred feet high using the same excavation procedures . . . ."

This was the common theme of much of the new evidence – the military's aggressive suppression of the story, which was obviously something that the destruction of a mere weather balloon was unlikely to provoke.

Frank Joyce was the announcer for local radio station KGFL back in 1947. He remembers the army's reaction to his interviewing Mac Brazel about what he had seen. Joyce took a wire recording of Brazel's story, intending to broadcast it the next day. That evening, soldiers visited the radio station and told Joyce and the station's owners that if they played the Brazel recording on air, they would have to look for a new line of work.

After Brazel had given this interview (his son Bill Brazel recalls), the rancher was kept in military custody for eight days. He was released briefly only once, to give another interview for KGFL. This time it was broadcast. The story that he now told on air was, according to Frank Joyce, very different from the original wire recording. Now Brazel sounded convinced that his find had, after all, only been a weather balloon.

Brazel's son told investigators that while in military detention, Brazel had sworn an oath not to reveal what he had seen that morning, and aside from confiding to his son that it was definitely not a weather balloon, he never had.

Investigators found quite a few people who mentioned the strange foil-like material, and the small humanoid aliens. They found many more who confirmed a military cover-up, backed by both veiled and direct threats. Even if the evidence of alien contact was tenuous and mainly confined to hearsay, the evidence of a harshly-enforced campaign of silence was widespread, first-hand and consistent.

Not all writers on UFOs were convinced that this was necessarily an alien spacecraft. In 1990, UFO expert John Keel suggested that the debris found by Brazel had been the remains of a Japanese balloon bomb. During the last year of World War II, the Japanese had been releasing cluster bombs attached to high altitude balloons, which would be carried east by the prevailing wind across the Pacific and over the United States.

In fact, Japanese balloon bombs were responsible for the only civilian deaths on US soil during World War II. During the summer of 1945, Reverend Archie Mitchell took his wife and some local children on a picnic in the Oregon woods. While he was busy parking the car, one of the children found a large balloon stuck in a tree. The bomb went off as they tried to get it down, killing the minister's wife and five of the children.

The US government had decided at the time that the deaths, and any other Japanese bomb balloons found, should be kept secret. They asked the media to cooperate. After all, they did not want the Japanese to know that their balloons were finding their targets – they would just send more. The strategy worked and the Japanese decided that all their balloons had been lost before they reached the US.

On the face of it, Japanese balloons seemed a plausible explanation of the Roswell Incident. Balloons trapped in the upper atmosphere can circulate for years before falling to earth. One might easily have fallen northwest of Roswell. But further research showed this to be unlikely. By 1947, it was unnecessary to keep the Japanese balloons a secret any more. Newspapers were referring to their recovery openly and knowledge of their existence was widespread.

Another all-inclusive explanation of both the wreckage and the bodies has been put forward by writer, Ron Schaffner. This centers on the activities of the rocket scientist, Werner von Braun. Could the craft have been an early space programme test flight crewed by monkeys? The crash could have burned of their hair and made them seem like tiny humanoids.

Nobody took this explanation very seriously. The declassified flight records from White Sands show no flights around the time of the Roswell crash. Furthermore, it is difficult to believe that anyone would mistake a monkey, burned or otherwise, for a space man.

Other theories, including one positing a prototype radar-deflecting stealth aircraft piloted by trained chimpanzees, were discussed and argued over by the ufological community. While everyone agreed that there had been a cover-up, few could agree on what it was supposed to be covering.

Then, in January 1994, Congressman Steven Schiff of Albuquerque, New Mexico, asked the US Government's General Accounting Office (GAO) to make a report on all documents referring to the Roswell incident. Congressman Schiff had pursued his interest in Roswell by asking questions of the Air Force. He felt that they were stonewalling him. The GAO proved more amenable, and they agreed to set about finding and examining both surviving documents and witnesses.

In fact, before the GAO could deliver its report, the Air Force (in what *Newsweek* described as "a preemptive strike") produced its own account of the evidence. The GAO's investigations had turned up some interesting material and the Air Force did not want to be accused of sitting on it.

But the 1994 United Stated Air Force (USAF) report was disappointing. In the first official word from the military on the subject of Roswell in 47 years, it derided the alien conspiracy theorists claiming that there was no evidence whatsoever for a cover-up. The survey carried out of USAF paperwork over the period, showed no increase in activity, secret or otherwise, during 1947.

The report allowed the slim possibility that a seamless cover-up might have forever hidden the evidence. However, the USAF pointed out that, over the same period, Top Secret details of the United States' nuclear program had been leaked to the Soviets. If the US government could hide information so well, why not use the technique to hide nuclear information that threatened the future of the world? It sounded a convincing argument.

However, one new detail did emerge, one that some would argue cast doubt on the rest of the report. While sticking to their story that the Roswell object was a balloon, the USAF offered the possibility that it was a different sort of balloon. It seemed that during 1947, a Top Secret project was being run jointly in New Mexico by the Air Force and New York University. Its name was "Project Mogul." Scientists from the university built and tested balloons designed to detect the shock waves generated by nuclear explosions. In the days before surveillance satellites, the balloons would also have provided a method of spying on the USSR's progress in developing nuclear weapons. Naturally, the US government wanted this project kept secret, and if a Mogul balloon crashed off military land there would be a security risk.

On the face of it, this certainly sounds like an all-encompassing and believable explanation. It takes in the balloon evidence and also gives a reason for a cover-up. It is the latter admission that raises doubt. Throughout the early part of the report, the USAF debunked a cover-up by arguing that no such operation could go on without leaving a paper trail through government files. Yet "Project Mogul" had all but disappeared from the files. The report states that full details of the project were only reconstructed during the 1994 investigations.

Of course, the beauty of the "Project Mogul" explanation is that, if it were true, General Ramey, Warrant Officer Irving Newton and all of the others who pronounced the Roswell find to be a weather balloon need not have been lying. They could have just mistaken one sort of balloon for another. On the surface this all sounds very plausible.

However, if the Roswell object was a "Project Mogul" balloon, we are still faced with some puzzling questions. If Ramey and the others were covering for the secret project, why do no records of the cover-up exist in the files? And if, alternatively, General Ramey thought that the Roswell object really was a weather balloon, why were the people of Roswell threatened to keep quiet?

There is a certain amount of evidence to support the "Project Mogul" theory. For example, many witnesses interviewed by the USAF remembered the floral Scotch tape used to secure parts of the balloon. From their description, it sounds very like the lines of "alien symbols" seen by the young Jesse Marcel Jr, printed on the debris.

Shortly after the arrival of the USAF report, Congressman Schiff's GAO report was published. Its findings were virtually identical. However, one interesting detail had somehow escaped the USAF. Roswell Army Air Field, like all other military installations, kept records of its communications with the rest of the military. During their investigations the GAO found that Roswell's outgoing message records from December 1946 through to October 1949 had been mysteriously destroyed. The GAO was unable to discover who had authorised the destruction, and why . . . .

In January 1994, while Congressman Schiff was interrogating the GAO, a small video production company in London announced that it had in its possession a remarkable film. It supposedly showed the autopsy of a humanoid creature performed in Roswell in 1947. The company, "Merlin Communications," also claimed to have footage of the crash-site itself, of the recovery of the crashed spacecraft and of President Truman inspecting one of the dead aliens. The details were so fantastic that most people assumed that it was a hoax and ignored it . . . .

Soon, stills from the film were offered for sale to news media. They were soon snapped up by tabloids in Europe – the *Morgen Post* in Germany and the *Sunday People* in the UK. Both papers printed brief accounts of the Roswell case next to the stills. And very strange stills they were.

They appeared to show a hairless, bloated creature, extremely similar to a human being. It was a gruesome sight, with a swollen belly and a gash on the right thigh. It appeared to have six members on its hands and feet and female genitalia. It lay on a white table in a white painted room and there were few objects around to judge scale by.

Interest from both the Ufological community and the general public was enormous. Greg Santilli, the head of

"Merlin Productions", plainly knew how to sell his property. It became known as the Santilli film, and it was learned that the photographic company Kodak had been asked to date the filmstock and had declared that it was almost certainly from 1947. Of course, this did not prove anything – the film could have remained unexposed until some hoaxer thought up the deception at a later date.

The Santilli film was shown on May 5, 1995, to an invited audience of media buyers and UFO investigators at the Museum of London in London's Barbican Center. They were searched for cameras, then they filed into the cinema and the lights went down.

What followed was both fascinating and horrific. The humanoid creature was slowly probed by two doctors. First, dark, rubbery inner lids were removed from the creatures eyes. Then, an incision was made from the neck to the belly and various indistinguishable internal organs were removed and stored in kidney dishes. The body seemed to ooze a black fluid. Unfortunately the cameraman seemed extremely inept. The picture was overexposed and none of the interesting details were in shot for more than an instant. All these features pointed to a hoax. Nevertheless, the body did not look like a model. The skin and musculature were extremely human. Many people present jumped to the conclusion that the "creature" was a doctored human corpse. Some outraged viewers called for a criminal investigation. In spite of all this, television stations from all over the world bought the film and included long sections in new documentaries on the Roswell case. Yet the larger the audience it reached, the greater became the general feeling that it was a hoax.

Doctors delivered the opinion that many of the abnormalities of the corpse were consistent with human medical conditions. The bloating of the limbs and abdomen (edema) are both associated with heart defects. The extra fingers and toes (polydactylism) are not as uncommon as one might think. In addition to these doubts, many Ufologists were simply incredulous about the film's provenance. The idea that the US government would seamlessly cover up everything else, then forget to reclaim a film of the actual alien, seemed ridiculous.

Santilli named the cameraman as Jack Barnett, but it seemed that this was a pseudonym. "Barnet's" story was that he had been asked by the military to film the operations at Roswell and had then been forgotten about. Without an officer to report to, Barnett had just hung on to the footage that he had shot. He could not be directly interviewed on the subject as he was in hiding, afraid of retribution for his sale of the film.

Kent Jeffrey, of the International Roswell Initiative, pointed out that if Barnett genuinely feared the consequences of his actions, his safest course would be to appear in the public eye as much as possible. That way, any attempt to prosecute him would be a public admission of the film's authenticity.

Research into the film has continued. One of the arguments against its authenticity was the presence in the background of a telephone with a "curly" wire. Arch-skeptic, Philip Klass, asserted that such wires were not used until 1956. Research by amateurs on the internet revealed an accredited photo from 1947 showing a "curly" wired phone.

When Japanese buyers of the film insisted on an interview with the cameraman, they received what no one else had, a film of him and some answers. He told the questioner that he had been present at the crash site and had seen the injured aliens cry out in pain as they died. "Barnett" explained the poor quality of the camera work by saying that he was forced to work around the doctors, and that he was wearing a heavy protective suit. Throughout the interview, "Barnett" referred to the creatures not as aliens or extraterrestrials but as "freaks". Santilli explained that the cameraman was a devout Christian and his beliefs would not allow him to accept that there was life on other planets. On the whole, the interview proved nothing and disproved nothing. It is true that "Barnett's" account of the recovery of the bodies matched many of the hearsay accounts dug up by UFO investigators. This could be because both the accounts and the interview deal with actual events. However, skeptics see it as a cynical attempt to fit in with previous false evidence.

While no one has yet proved the Santilli film a fake, most people who have seen it feel that it is unconvincing. But then, whether the film is real or a fake has no bearing on the major question. What crashed in the New Mexico desert 50 years ago and why did the military go to so much trouble to silence the witnesses?

The Death of Captain Thomas Mantell

The Roswell Incident only became a celebrated UFO case many years after it had happened. The US military's cover-up was, in the short-term at least, successful. However, if their aim was to suppress the saucer craze, they failed. Less than six months later, a UFO story broke that caught the interest of the world – the death of US pilot, Captain Thomas Mantell, while pursuing a UFO.

On January 7, 1948, the control tower at Godman Field near Fort Knox, Kentucky, was notified that a number of local residents had reported a UFO sighting. In fact, it was seen near the base that afternoon. Two hours later, at about 3.00 p.m., five P-51 Fighters (led by Captain Thomas Mantell) took off to investigate. Unfortunately, the planes did not possess oxygen cylinders and four of them dropped out as they passed the official limit of 14,000 feet for their type of aircraft. Mantell who had told the control tower that he was chasing a UFO that was "metallic and tremendous in size, and appears to be moving about half my speed" continued to chase it. He was last seen at 3.15 p.m., continuing to climb. This was the last that was heard from him. Nearly two hours later, at 5.00 p.m., the wreckage of his aircraft was found near Franklin, Kentucky. The time of the impact was recorded by his watch, which had stopped at 3.18 p.m.

It seemed obvious that Mantell had simply blacked out as he had run out of oxygen – he was well above 22,000 feet when he ceased to call the tower. But rumors soon spread that he had been shot down by a UFO. The Air Force made things worse by explaining that the UFO reported near the base had actually been the planet Venus, and then, realizing that this was implausible during the day, that it was a weather balloon.

On the whole, this explanation seems plausible. The fact that the object was moving at only half the speed of Mantell's aircraft and that those who saw it described it as white and "umbrella-shaped", makes it sound more like a weather balloon than the usual fast-moving UFO.

Saucers Over Europe

On January 7, 1954, at 4.26 a.m., M. Brevart, a baker at Arras in France, was working in his bakehouse when he thought he would step outside for a breath of fresh air. Scarcely had he done so than a strange glow in the sky made him look upwards. At a point just above the Place de la Vacquerie, behind the town hall, a luminous disc as big as the full moon (but much brighter) was hanging motionless. M. Brevart, startled and incredulous, rubbed his eyes but the object was undoubtedly there and apparently not very far above the town. It remained in this position for several seconds, and then suddenly started a rocking movement, discharged a dazzling flash of light which illuminated the whole of the Place and vanished at an immense speed in the direction of St Pol-sur-Ternoize, nearer the coast, filling the sky with an enormous orange-colored radiance.

"Almost at the same moment, at 7.27 a.m., a railwayman who was on duty at Orchies, about 25 miles northeast of Arras as the crow flies, saw a shining disc vanishing towards the southwest. It was moving horizontally at an enormous speed, with the vivid orange-colored light trailing behind it.

"A few seconds later the whole of the Seine-Inférieure department from Fécamp in the west to Dieppe in the north, Mailleraye in the south to Gournay in the east, was lit up by what seemed to be a huge fire in the sky. For half a minute the light was so bright that the railwaymen at Serqueux were able to see the registration numbers of the carriages. A few minutes later, Dieppe was suddenly shaken by a tremendous explosion which smashed a large number of windows and woke up most of the people in the town.

"That evening a spokesman of the Astrophysical Institute of Paris made the following statement, 'It is very probable that the phenomenon seen this morning in the Dieppe area was a meteorite.'"

The Institute failed to explain why the meteorite was hanging suspended above the Town Hall.

This incident is recorded by the first of the major French Flying Saucer experts, Aimé Michel, in a book called *The Truth About Flying Saucers* (1956). The distinguished man of letters, Jean Cocteau, provided an introduction. Like Charles Fort, he took the opportunity to thumb his nose at authority. "We must hope that the new satellites observed 600 kilometers from our globe in the last few months are not the checkpoints and artificial garages of these swift and silent vehicles. We must also hope that the whole thing remains a theory and will not humble the pride which blinds mankind and leaves it to think that what it does not know is impossible."

Michel's book is an excellent history of UFO sightings until that time – beginning with Kenneth Arnold, but also including a number of earlier ones. The most interesting part of his book is the second half, where he writes at length about all the important sightings so far over Europe. Many of these were seen in the clear skies of Africa. A report from Bocaranga on November 22, 1952, is typical of them. Father Carlos Maria had hitched a lift with a businessman from Bouar to go and see his dentist. Father Carlos describes how in a tree-lined road at dusk, "we suddenly saw a large disc which seemed to be about to traverse the sky ahead and was rather low down." This disappeared but sometime afterwards, they were obliged to stop to refuel. At this point, eight of them were able to see "four discs hanging in the sky to the left of the road. We could see them quite clearly, although it was impossible to judge their distance. There were two above and two below, and they were not in contact. When they came to a standstill they were pale silver in color, like the moon.

"I had several opportunities of seeing them in motion and had a strong idea that the lower pair only were revolving. Just before moving, they blazed up as bright as the sun. Then they seemed to arrange themselves in a group which proceeded to describe circles before returning to their starting point. When they stopped, the bright blaze died down to the original dull silver . . . . we were watching them from 10.00 to 10.20 p.m. After their final circling movement, they remained motionless for several minutes. Then they departed and disappeared in the opposite direction to ours, still keeping to the left of the road. Such at least was my impression, but I do not rule out the possibility that they might never have moved and that I might have been deceived by a gradual diminution of luminosity until they were lost in the darkness of the night."

Michel goes on to consider Father Carlos Maria's story at considerable length, carefully examining every detail. Then, in the logical manner of the French, he does his best to explain it with a theory. This theory is not his own, but that of one "Lieutenant Plantier", "one of the most brilliant brains in the new French Air Force." Bored to death in a minor post, Lieutenant Plantier devoted his mind to the problem of inventing a machine capable of escaping the gravitational pull of the earth. Jet propelled rockets, he thought, were crude and wasteful. Surely it ought to be possible to make use of the energy of cosmic rays, the radiation that reaches earth from some unknown point in space, which seems to consist largely of highly charged protons moving at a very high speed. These, says Lieutenant Plantier, contain energy amounting to about 100,000 times the energy to split an atomic nucleus.

Plantier's idea was that it ought to be possible to transform the energy of cosmic rays into energies of a lower kind – "like the blow of the hammer upon the anvil, which transforms kinetic energy into calorific energy."

Plantier's next question was, "suppose you were asked to invent a machine that would transform cosmic rays into 'usable energy,' where would you start?" He mentions a device called the "photometric propeller" which revolves because one side of its blades is painted black, and black absorbs light while the other, painted white, does not. "Light sails" on spacecraft make use of the same principle and are driven by a hail of photons from the sun.

If a machine could be created which absorbed this cosmic energy and could make use of it, it would be driven along on exactly the same principle as a photometric propeller. "There would be thus a kind of continuous jet, pulsating right through the machine. Released by the machine, it would follow it on its journey, propel it, and hold it up when it stopped, very like the jets of water on which ping-pong balls are poised in shooting galleries at fairs." Plantier then went on to say, "to achieve its full efficiency, the machine must be in the form of a disc which is perfectly symmetrical in relation to its axis." Moreover, "the machine could travel at the most terrifying speeds without producing a sound, and break through the sound barrier without producing the transonic bang." This is because the force field of the machine would drag the surrounding air along with it. Each successive layer of air would drag the next layer along with it at a slightly slower speed, and so on. This would mean that "the machine could move through the atmosphere at enormous speeds without experiencing any increase of temperature." And since the machine contains a field of force which includes the passengers, the passengers would not notice the tremendous acceleration, even if it went at thousands of miles an hour.

Michel goes on, "Lieutenant Plantier had reached this point in his reasoning when a crazy notion entered his head, a notion which I am sure has entered the reader's – his impossible contrivance, a brainchild born of the boredom of an outlandish military station, *already existed*. He had seen it. It was the flying saucer."

According to Plantier, his machine would have to oscillate for a fraction of a second and then tilt at "a very marked angle" in order to take off. This, he says, has been observed in the case of flying saucers. He worked out that this tilting of the machine would be accomplished by a screen inside it, capable of changing position. The movements of this screen would be visible outside the machine in the form of a patch of light below it – again, something that many observers of flying saucers have noticed. Above the machine, Plantier calculated, there would probably be a patch of cloud, even in a completely blue sky, because the field of force would cause an upward rush of air above the machine which would produce condensation. Plantier describes a UFO sighting by an Air Force pilot called Réne Sacle on

December 29, 1952, at Courcon-d'Aunis, Charente-Maritime, who saw, to his amazement, a lonely little cumulonimbus cloud rise vertically in the clear blue sky and then cast off something vague and shapeless which rapidly disappeared, leaving a white trail behind it.

3

Alien Contact

While most of the world seemed to be seeing saucers in the sky, some people were getting a closer look . . . .

On July 23, 1947, a group of survey workers at Bauru, in Brazil, saw a large metallic disc settle down on curved legs not far from them. All but one took to their heels. The man who remained, Jose Higgins, claims that he found himself face to face with three seven-foot-tall humanoids, all wearing transparent overalls, with metal boxes on their backs. He claims that they had large bald heads, big round eyes, no eyebrows, and long legs. After this, they dug some holes in the ground and began throwing large boulders about. From the position of the holes in the ground, Higgins guessed that they were trying to indicate the position of planets with regard to the sun and noticed that they pointed with particular insistence at the seventh of these holes. It was later speculated that they were trying to indicate that they came from the planet Uranus. After this, they reentered their craft, which took off with a great whistling noise. The account appeared in two Brazilian newspapers.

Three weeks later, on August 14, 1947, a professor named Johannis was walking in the mountains near

Friuli, Italy, when he saw a large metallic disc, and two dwarf-like creatures (less than three feet tall), wearing translucent blue overalls with red collars and belts. Johannis claims that when he waved an alpine pick at them, one of them raised a hand to his belt, which emitted a puff of smoke, and caused the pick to fly out of the professor's hand. One of the "spacemen" then took the pick and they retreated into their craft, which shot into the air.

Three days later, in Death Valley, California, two prospectors witnessed what seemed to be the crash-landing of a flying saucer, and saw two small beings emerge from it. Chased by the prospectors, they vanished amongst the sand dunes and when the prospectors went back, the craft had disappeared.

But it was in 1953 that the most sensational account so far of "alien contact" was published. It was a book called *Flying Saucers Have Landed*, by George Adamski and a journalist named Desmond Leslie. Adamski, who was a counter assistant at a hamburger bar on the slopes of Mount Palomar – the home of the great observatory – and who awarded himself the honorary degree of "professor," claimed to have been seeing UFOs since 1946 – that is, a year before Kenneth Arnold. He also claimed that on March 5, 1951, he had photographed a giant cigar-shaped craft surrounded by smaller UFOs which had emerged from it, and had taken another similar picture in the following year.

Adamski stated that on November 20, 1952, he had accompanied six friends into the California desert. These included another author called George H. Williamson, also a writer on flying saucers, who was to claim in one of his books that UFOs were stabled in a hangar under the Great Pyramid, which was built by spacemen 24,000 years ago.

According to Adamski, his hunch that they would be granted a "sighting" was justified when, "riding high, and without sound, there was a gigantic cigar-shaped silvery ship, without wings or appendages of any kind." Adamski asked to be taken down the road, and his companions then returned to their original parking spot. When a number of aircrafts suddenly appeared and circled the cigar-shaped ship, it turned and vanished. But at this point, Adamski saw a flash in the sky and "a beautiful craft appeared to be drifting through a saddle between two of the mountain peaks." Adamski then saw a man beckoning to him from the opening of a ravine, and as he approached him, realised that he was looking at a visitor from another world.

The alien had "wavy shoulder length sandy hair, and suntanned skin." He had a high forehead, calm grey green eyes that slanted, high cheek bones, and "a finely chiselled" nose. He was wearing a brown single-piece suit.

Communicating telepathically, the alien explained that he was from the planet Venus, and after a conversation, he was picked up by a flying saucer and flew away. Adamski's six companions, who then joined him, found a footprint in the sand. The alien returned a month later, and this time Adamski was allowed to take photographs of the saucer which he reproduced in his book.

This became an instant bestseller and Adamski lost no time in following it up with a book called *Inside the Flying Saucers* (1955), in which he described how the aliens had taken him on a trip around the moon and how he had seen rivers and lakes on its far side – the side which is permanently turned away from the earth.

Adamski's preposterous stories took in a surprising

number of people. His coauthor, Desmond Leslie, was later to admit that when he coauthored *Flying Saucers Have Landed*, he had never met him. "My publisher and I both agreed that there was sufficient evidence in his testimony that he had contacted a flying saucer on the ground, to warrant publishing his narrative. Later events proved that we were justified . . . ." And in a later book, *Flying Saucers Farewell* (1961), another flying saucer enthusiast, C. A. Honey, (who had known Kenneth Arnold), announced his total belief in Adamski – whom he claimed was "distinguished as a college professor" – and who claimed that the US State Department was trying to cover up its knowledge of the reality of flying saucers.

Adamski died in 1965 – at the age of 78 – and so succeeded in escaping the discrediting he deserved when the age of space flight revealed that the backside of the moon was as bleak as its front and that the temperature on Venus was far too high to sustain life.

Adamski's success made more "alien contacts" inevitable. In a book called *Aboard a Flying Saucer* (1953), Truman Bethurum described meeting little green men – or at least, olive men – who wore uniforms and came from a planet called Clarion which is permanently hidden behind the moon.

He also met an incredibly beautiful woman called Aura Rhanes who spent the night with him – disappointingly, only in conversation. Daniel Fry described meeting an alien in the desert in New Mexico whose English was so good that he was able to warn Fry, "better not touch the hull, pal. It's still hot." His purpose, he explained, was to persuade Fry to write a book warning earth men about prospects of a future nuclear war.

In *The Secret of the Flying Saucers* (1955), Orfeo Ange-lucci described making a flight to Neptune and discover-ing that he had been one of the space aliens in a previous existence. Howard Menger, in *From Outer Space to You* (1959), enlivens his account of aliens with descriptions of a number of beautiful blondes, one of whom was over 500 years old. Another contactee, Marian Keech, also claimed to have met beings from the planet Clarion and Jesus – who had changed his name to Sananda – ex-plained that he had also moved there. The purpose of the visit was to warn the earth people that a great flood was about to wipe out Salt Lake City, and all who wished to escape it should take to the higher ground. This pro-phecy seemed to echo the end-of-the-world prophecies of the nineteenth century – and, like them, was discre-dited when the disaster failed to occur.

One contactee called George King, a London taxi driver, described how he was alone in his flat when he was told that he was going to become the voice of an Interplanetary Parliament. After several trips to Mars and Venus, and saving the earth from destruction by helping to intercept a meteor, he moved to California where his "Aetherius Society" has become one of the most success-ful organizations of its kind.

Yet some alien contacts had what would later be recognized as the stamp of authenticity. On March 22, 1953, two lesbians who preferred to call themselves Sarah Shaw and Jan Whitley saw a bright light sweeping back and forth across their house in Tujunga Canyon, Califor-nia. As Sarah knelt on the bed to peer out of the window, she felt giddy and confused. When she looked at the clock again, she realized that more than two hours had gone past, and that it was now after 4.00 a.m.

It was not until 1975, when Sarah agreed to hypnosis, that she recalled that she and Jan had been taken from their cabin and floated up through the air on to a UFO. There they were undressed and examined by black clad aliens who told Sarah that vinegar was a cure for cancer. Sarah apparently enjoyed the attentions she received from the male aliens. They were then "floated" back to their cabin, where they lost all memory of the encounter.

Although the "psychic investigator" Scott Rogo was to conclude that the symbolic rape was due to Sarah's unconscious dissatisfaction with her lesbian relationship, the events followed the pattern that would be later described by a great many UFO "abductees." The Sarah and Jan case seems to be the first on record.

On August 21, 1955, Billy Ray Taylor and his wife June were visiting their friend Elmer Sutton on his farm near Hopkinsville, Kentucky. At about 7.00 p.m., Billy went out into the yard to fetch a drink from the well and saw a strange craft, "real bright, but with an exhaust all the colors of the rainbow" land in a gulch nearby. Oddly enough, the Sutton family failed to be excited by his report and no one bothered to go outside.

An hour later, they were all alerted by the barking of the dog to the presence of an intruder near the farmhouse, and saw "a small glowing man with extremely large eyes, his arms extended over his head." The two Sutton men fired at him with a rifle and shotgun and there was a sound "as if I'd shot into a bucket," and the spaceman turned and hurried off. When another visitor appeared at the window the rifle was again fired and they ran outside to see if the creature had been hit. As one of them stopped under a low portion of the roof, a claw-like hand reached down from it and touched his hair. More shots were fired at the creature on the roof, and although it was hit directly, it floated to the ground and hurried away. For the next three hours, the 11 occupants of the house remained behind bolted doors frequently seeing the "spacemen" at the windows. Finally, they rushed out of the house, piled into two cars and drove to the nearest policestation in Hopkinsville. The police who returned with them could find no sign of the spacemen, but as soon as they were gone the creatures reappeared. The next day, a police artist got witnesses to describe what they had seen. The picture that emerged were of tiny creatures with egg-shaped heads, very large yellow eyes spaced wide apart and huge elephant-like ears. Their long thin arms ended in claw-like hands. They had slim, straight silvery bodies that seemed to be lit from the inside. This inner light, the Suttons said, intensified whenever they were shot at or even shouted at.

In spite of the derision that their story aroused when reported in the press, the Suttons – and the Taylors – continued to insist on its truth and serious investigators who questioned them had no doubt whatever that they were not inventing their story.

On October, 15, 1957, Antonio Villa Boas from Minas Gerais, Brazil, had an extremely Close Encounter of the Third Kind. Villa Boas, a farmer's son, was out ploughing in his tractor one evening, when he saw a red light descending out of the sky toward him. As it approached, he saw that it was an egg-shaped craft with purple lights twinkling around its horizontal circumference. Terrified, Villa Boas tried to drive away in his tractor. As the craft got closer the engine died. As he tried to run away across the ploughed field, Villa Boas was grabbed by three small humanoid creatures and pulled into the craft.

Inside, Villa Boas found himself in a small, bright, metal room, staring at a group of creatures like those who had grabbed him. Spherical helmets obscured their faces. He could only see their eyes, which glowed blue. The creatures stripped Villa Boas naked and led him to another room, which smelt so rank that he vomited. There, they took a blood sample and rubbed his naked body down with a sponge. Then they left him alone.

After half an hour, the door opened and Villa Boas was amazed to see a beautiful, naked woman enter the room. She appeared to be human in all features, except her pubic hair which was bright red. Villa Boas described her as "more beautiful than any [woman] that I have ever seen." Showing incredible fortitude, Villa Boas immediately had sex with the woman who seemed very willing. However, when he tried again as soon as they had finished she was less enthusiastic.

She patted her stomach then pointed upwards. Villa Boas took this to mean that she would bear his child back on the aliens' native planet. His clothes were returned and he was dropped off back in the ploughed field. Feeling slightly used, he watched the craft disappear into the night.

The Betty Andreasson Abduction

On January 25, 1967, Betty Ann Andreasson of South Ashburnam, Massachusetts, was cooking dinner when all the lights in her kitchen went out. In fact, all the lights in the house had gone out and soon her seven children, aged between three and 11 rushed into the kitchen. As their eyes became used to the dark, they could see a pulsating orange glow coming through the small kitchen window. Betty was frightened and pushed her children out of the room.

Meanwhile, Waino Aho, Betty's father had come to see what was going on. Waino was temporarily the only man in the house, as Betty's husband James was in the hospital following a serious car crash. Thus it was Waino who approached the window to see what was happening.

Outside on the grass, Waino saw a procession of small, humanoid creatures. He described them later as looking like "Halloween freaks". They were crossing the lawn towards the house, jumping like grasshoppers one after the other. As they got nearer, the leader of the column looked up and saw Waino. Meeting the creature's eyes, he felt strange. In fact, all of the family (except Betty) began to feel strange. With one exception they remember nothing of what happened from that point on. Betty herself rushed to the door to see what was approaching. She did not have to wait long to find out.

Passing through the door, as though it was not there, the line of creatures entered the Andreasson's hallway. Naturally, Betty was stunned and groping for an explanation, turned to her fundamentalist Christian faith. She realized that the creatures must be angels. They were flat-faced and gray-skinned, standing about four feet high. Their leader, who had stared at Waino, was slightly taller. Their eyes were long and almond-shaped and all of one light cloudy colour. They were wearing uniforms of a shiny blue material, with a sash across the chest. On their arms was a small insignia that looked like a bird with outstretched wings.

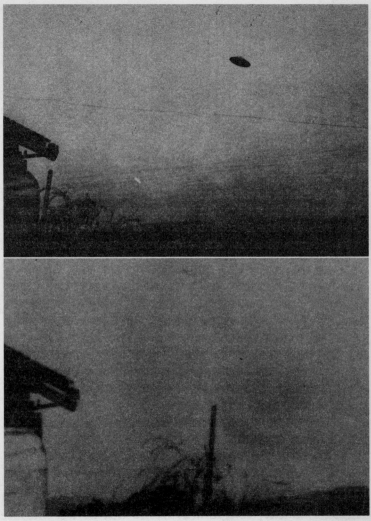

A UFO photographed by farmer Paul Trent over his farm on November 5, 1950

Betty heard a voice in her head that seemed to come from the leader. She got the impression that his name was "Quazgaa." The creature held out its hand to her and Betty understood by this that they were hungry. In a kind of trance, she led them back to the kitchen and began to cook some meat on the stove.

The creatures seemed puzzled and told her that they could only eat food that had been burned. Betty let the meat burn and the creatures watched in amazement as smoke from the pan rose into the air. The creatures seemed to realize that Betty had misunderstood. They tried again. They explained that she had misunderstood. Their food was knowledge, knowledge "tried by fire." They asked if Betty had anything like that.

Once again, Betty's Christian faith provided the answer and she led the creatures to the front room. Sat around the TV, where their mother had sent them, Betty's seven children sat as still as stone. It was as though time had stopped for everyone except Betty and the creatures. Betty picked up her Bible, the only "knowledge tried by fire" that she could think of and gave it to the leader. In return, Quazgaa handed her a thin blue book. Watching in amazement, Betty saw Quazgaa wave his hand over the Bible. New copies of the book appeared from nowhere. Quazgaa gave these to his companions. They were thicker than the original volume and each page glowed brilliant white. For a moment, the group of creatures stood reading the Bibles, the pages flipping by as though blown by the wind.

At about this time, Betty Andreasson's 11-year-old daughter, Becky, temporarily came out of her trance. She saw Quazgaa holding a book, and noticed that the TV was still on although the picture had faded into a pattern of grays. The creatures scared the child and Quazgaa seems to have become aware of this. As it turned to look at Becky, she lapsed back into her trance.

While this was happening, Betty had been looking in the book that Quazgaa had given her. The pages glowed like those of the duplicated Bibles. Inside, there were abstract pictures made up of coils and wheels. Coming to the end of the book, Betty looked up into Quazgaa's eyes. They had changed from cloudy to black. In her mind, Betty heard the question "Will you follow us?"

For a moment Betty was worried. She now doubted that her visitors were angels and she was afraid for her family. Quazgaa reassured her that her family would be fine. In their trances they looked peaceful. Betty also felt herself to be in a kind of trance, as though her fear was being sucked out of her. In this state, she agreed to go with them.

Betty followed the line of creatures back out into the garden, passing through the closed door as she went. The group proceeded as before, in slow jumps. At the end of her garden, Betty was amazed to see a huge shiny disc standing on thin metal legs. Sensing her fear, Quazgaa reassured her that there was nothing dangerous inside. Then, to Betty's amazement, she suddenly became able to see through the metal of the saucer's base. Inside she recognized some of the shapes she had seen in the thin blue book. Especially interesting was a mechanism that Betty seemed to recognize as the ship's propulsion system. It consisted of three or four large skittle shaped objects, connected in a ring.

Despite the weirdness of this experience, Betty remained calm. It was as though Quazgaa was stifling her fear by using the mental link between them. Reassured, Betty followed as the creatures jumped up to a door that had opened in the side of the saucer. Inside, Betty found herself in a room with curved walls. Quazgaa and the others withdrew slightly from her and seemed to be having a discussion. While they spoke, Betty began to feel odd. Her limbs seemed to be weightless and she felt very tired. Finally, two of the creatures broke away from the group and led Betty to another room, leaving Quazgaa behind. They glided along as before, one creature in front and another behind.

Led like a prisoner, and yet still curiously calm, Betty was taken up a flight of stairs to the ship's upper deck. This room was circular and domed, with a pattern of leaf-like objects on the walls. Areas of the wall seemed to ripple and reflect light. While staring at the odd ripples, Betty realized that she was being left behind. She asked the creatures why, but they told her that she was to stay there. As she "heard" this, Betty found that she was unable to move. The creatures left.

Paralysed and alone, Betty began to become very scared. As she waited helplessly, the lighting in the room became brighter and brighter. Suddenly an opening appeared in the wall, telescoping outwards like an old-fashioned camera. Then two creatures appeared through the opening and asked Betty to come with them. With the creatures standing either side of her, Betty was lead to the center of the room. There, the trio sank through the floor and floated down a transparent tube to another circular room.

Betty was led to a platform below a bright light. The creatures told Betty that the light would cleanse her. As she stepped onto it, the platform rose up and into the bright halo of light above. After a few moments it descended again and Betty was led to a small cubicle. The creatures asked her to undress. Betty protested, but the creatures just kept asking. Finally she agreed. In the cubicle was an all-over garment, like a cloak with short sleeves. It had small slits on the bottom hem at the back and sides. It was open up the front and fastened at the neck with a butterfly-shaped transparent button. It was made of a plastic-like material with sealed edges, as though it had been cut with hot shears.

As she stepped out of the cubicle, Betty again became scared. She prayed to Jesus to help her as, gliding in line, the creatures led her to a huge domed room. At its center was a long box. To Betty it looked just like an operating table. At this, she panicked and screamed "No!". Quazgaa entered the room. As she screamed her protests, Betty floated over onto the table. The creatures clustered around her. Their flesh seemed somehow whiter than it had in under the lights of her kitchen.

One of the creatures took a thin silver needle and slid it up Betty's left nostril. She could hear tissue tearing as it penetrated further and further. At the same time, another needle was being pushed through her belly button into her abdomen. Wriggling to escape and feeling terrible pain, Betty found that once again she was paralysed. Just as the experience was becoming unbearable, Quazgaa reached over and touched Betty's forehead. With that, the pain subsided. The creatures seemed puzzled by their examination of Betty's abdomen. They kept mentioning "creation." Betty realised that they were fruitlessly looking for her womb – Betty had undergone a hysterectomy.

Finally the examination was over and the needles were removed. As she watched the creatures pull the needle from her nose, Betty noticed that it had something attached to the end, a bloody ball covered in tiny spikes. It had not been there when the needle was inserted. Clearly the object had been in her sinus to begin with. She was then returned to the dressing cubicle and there changed back into her clothes. Some of the terror of the examination had subsided now, and she joined her two companions with her sense of hypnotic calm restored. It was not to last long.

The creatures led Betty through a door and down a dark tunnel to a cylindrical room lined on either side with large chairs. They asked Betty to sit in one of them. A glass-like cover pivoted down over her, sealing her into the chair. The cover fitted closely preventing movement, as though it had been vacuum-moulded. At the level of the mouth and nostrils, three vents in the cover connected to tubes that extended into the ceiling.

The creatures instructed her to close her eyes and when she did, she found herself unable to open them again. As she waited fearfully, Betty felt a liquid begin to pour over her head. The space between the cover and the chair rapidly filled with the liquid, forcing Betty to breathe through the vents. As the liquid crept up her body, waves of relaxation and contentment flowed through her. Soon she became unconscious.

When she awoke, Betty had the sense that they had travelled a great distance. As she looked around her, the cover of the chair lifted off and she was once again joined by the two small creatures. Over their heads and faces they wore black hoods. Betty noticed that her clothes had somehow dried off. The trio walked down a tunnel along a narrow path. The darkness was lit only by a faint glow from the creatures' suits. After some minutes, they emerged onto what seemed to be the surface of a planet or perhaps the floor of some enormous cave. Betty could see nothing except the floor, the path and the atmosphere which was red, tinting everything.

Soon she could see two large buildings looming out of the red haze on either side of the path. They were square and tall, rather like tower blocks. As they passed between them, Betty was horrified to see that the walls of the building were crawling with grotesque creatures. They resembled hairless monkeys. Instead of a head, each creature had two dark eyes on stalks that grew directly from the shoulders. The buildings continued on either side as they glided on. The monkey-like creatures watched them impassively. Betty's hooded companions paid them no attention.

As they passed from the "town," the path began to curve upwards on an elevated piece of land. As they climbed, the atmosphere abruptly became green, as though they had passed from one distinct layer to another. The creatures took off their hoods. Other paths, like the one they were on, criss-crossed in the air. Below them, Betty could see other buildings. One looked like an irregular pyramid with white edges. Others were domed. Ahead, in the air around the path, floated vast crystalline objects, spheres and ovoids, reflecting and refracting light in all the colors of the rainbow. Passing among these, Betty could see a bright light in front of them that blocked the path.

As she watched the light, Betty began to see something taking shape before it. Soon she could see that it was a giant bird, like an eagle, with its wings outstretched, blocking out the light. As they approached, Betty began to feel warmer. The temperature rose until they were very near the bird. Just as it was becoming unbearable, it subsided.

Opening her eyes (which she had closed against the heat), Betty could see that the bird had burned to a pile of ashes before them. As she watched, the ashes writhed into the form of a fat, gray worm. The air was filled with the smell of incense. Betty sensed that this strange vision was what she had been brought to see. Hesitantly, she asked the creature if it was Jesus. It replied that God was love and that it loved her. It told her that it did not desire to harm her and that any pain she had felt was a product of her own fear. Then, as if to confirm the Christian link, the creature told her that she could only lose that fear "through my son."

This seemed to be what the aliens wanted to tell Betty. From the bright light in the sky, Betty and the creatures retraced their journey across the planet of the red and green atmospheres back to the room of chairs. There she was once again put into a restful sleep. When she awoke, they returned to the saucer where Betty once again met Quazgaa.

Staring into her eyes, the alien commander's pupils became very large. One was black, the other white. Telepathically, he told Betty that she was to be given formulae and that there would be no further contact until humans had understood these. Humankind, Quazgaa said, was obsessed with the physical and had pushed science as far as it could go in the study of physical phenomena. Yet they had almost entirely neglected the spiritual. Some of the answers, he said, lay in the study of fire. There is energy, "the simplest form of energy," present in the atmosphere around us. "Man knows nothing of this as yet." Quazgaa also told Betty that, for the moment, she would forget her experiences and that they would only resurface later in her life at an appointed time. With that, Betty was sent back to her two companions. Assuming her familiar position between them, they floated with her out of the ship and back onto her fog-covered lawn.

Betty Andreasson remembered these bizarre experiences in 1975 and wrote to Dr Allen Hynek, the eminent ufologist. At the time, Hynek was snowed under with similar letters and he left the letter unconsidered for some time. Rereading it, however, he became convinced that Betty Andreasson was a sincere person genuinely in need of help to understand her "experiences." Ufologists, Raymond Fowler and Dr Harold Edelstein, contacted Betty and offered to investigate her claims using hypnotic regression. Both Betty and her daughter Becky agreed to this. The above account was summarized from the many sessions of hypnosis that took place over the course of 1977. Betty's father, Waino Aho, signed an affidavit covering his memories of the UFO's landing and the creatures' arrival.

Betty Andreasson's close encounter resembles other abduction cases closely in most of its details, the medical examination is common to a great number of accounts. It is where the story differs, however, that is most intriguing. The burning bird and its quasi-Christian speech seem just too weird to be anything other than a devout believer's strange dream. Yet who is to say what is normal in such an abnormal experience? It is possible that Betty Andreasson rationalized her experiences using a familiar frame of reference – her religious convictions. The incident in which she misunderstood Quazgaa's request for "burned food" illustrates that the aliens' mental communication often came across as vague and metaphoric.

The phoenix, the mythological animal that Betty's vision closely resembled, was supposed to have burned to ashes in dying. These ashes transformed into a worm. The phoenix is a pagan symbol not associated in the modern mind with Christ. Yet Raymond Fowler, who thoroughly investigated every aspect of the testimony, discovered that the phoenix had in fact been an early Christian symbol, appropriated from Classical myth to symbolise Christ's resurrection. Could Betty Andreasson have been aware of this little-known fact?

Hypnotic regression is a controversial subject itself, even when used to unearth more everyday facts. Its use in investigating child abuse long after the event has been severely criticized. Psychologists point out that what is recovered it often a cocktail of fact and imagination, or alternatively a product of the interviewer's expectations and prompting. On this last count, at least, the Andreasson investigators can be exonerated. Examination of the session transcripts shows that they carefully avoided all leading questions.

Supported as it is by the testimonies of three people, one of whom did not undergo hypnosis, the Andreasson abduction cannot be written off as solely a product of a wild imagination. Dr Allen Hynek, to whom Betty Andreasson first wrote, has described abduction stories in general as being characterised by "high strangeness." It would be difficult to find a better example of this than the whole Andreasson affair.

The Travis Walton Abduction

At just after 6.00 p.m. on November 5, 1975, seven woodsmen were returning from their day's work in the Apache-Sitgreaves National Forest in Arizona. They worked with chainsaws, thinning away unwanted trees to give the chosen saplings a chance to grow. It was hard work and they were all exhausted as their pickup truck bounced down the rutted track back to their hometown of Heber.

Suddenly one of the woodsmen, Travis Walton, noticed a light filtering through the trees to the right of the road. At first he thought it was a dying ray of the sun. Then he realised that the sun had set at least half an hour before. He pointed it out to his friends and they were intrigued. All seven were staring out of the right window when they drew level with the source of the light.

At first it seemed to be a crashed plane, burning brightly in the upper branches of a tall tree. Yet it did not flicker. It dawned on them that they were looking at a flying saucer. It was shaped like two pie-dishes turned rim to rim, with a hemispherical bulge on top. Judging by the trees around it, it was perhaps 20 feet in diameter and ten feet tall. It gave off a golden glow. On the forest floor beneath it, cut logs and underbrush cast strange shadows in its eerie light.

The truck slowed to a stop as its occupants stared in disbelief. In that second, Travis Walton decided that he wanted a closer look. Thrown out of their reverie by the snap of the passenger door opening, his co-workers watched in terror as Walton jumped from the truck and began sneaking towards the ship, ducking behind

73

logs, trying to stay hidden. They shouted for him to stop. They wanted to drive off, to get as far away as possible from the weird shape that hung above them. Yet Travis was making his way closer and closer to the object. They watched him in an agony of indecision.

Walton was, by now, close enough to see that the surface of the saucer was totally smooth, mistily reflecting the trees around it. Its light seemed to be coming from a line of panels around the base. Suddenly the saucer began to wobble, emitting as it did so a deep swelling sound like a vast generator starting up. Travis thought that the ship had noticed him and was about to fly off. When it just continued to wobble and groan, Walton decided to make a run for it back to the truck.

His six workmates saw him stand up from his hiding place. At that instant, a sea-green ray, 12 inches wide, shot from the base of the craft and struck Walton in the chest. It made a curious popping sound. Walton was smashed upward and backward by the impact. He flew about ten feet. His friends in the truck could not stand any more. In a panic, the driver stamped on the accelerator and the pickup screeched off down the bumpy track . . . .

Walton had been knocked unconscious. He had not even seen what hit him. Gradually he began to come to. He ached all over. Opening his eyes, he saw a luminous panel above him. He was lying on his back staring at the ceiling which seemed to be made of brushed metal. The air was warm and humid. He seemed to be lying on some sort of table. Moving his shoulders, Walton could feel that his jacket and shirt had been pulled up around his chest. Something heavy pressed down on his torso. He imagined that he must be in hospital, badly injured. The

74

doctors had not even had time to undress him.

Looking down, Walton saw that the weight on his chest was a dark gray metal object, about five inches thick. It enclosed his upper torso, like some kind of scanner. Was he coming out of anaesthetic in the middle of an operation? In the periphery of his vision, Walton saw three figures that he assumed were his doctors. They seemed to be examining him. Summoning all his strength, he lifted his head and focussed his attention on one of his attendants.

They were not human! They were small (about five feet tall), with smooth, pudgy white flesh. They seemed to have no body hair. Their heads were curiously child-like, large braincases with underdeveloped features. The only exception to this were the eyes, which were huge and glassy. Walton found himself staring into a pair of pupils that were over an inch across. Galvanized by panic, Walton jerked into a sitting position, throwing the gray metal device off his chest. He struck out to clear a path for himself, hitting one of the creatures standing to his right. Through its one piece suit, the alien felt soft and boneless. Still aching, Walton heaved himself off the table.

The creatures stood just out of his reach, waiting. By the table, Walton noticed a bench covered in strange implements. He grabbed what looked like a serviceable club – a long transparent tube. As soon as he had it in his hands, Walton realised that it was far too light to do any real damage. Nevertheless, he swung it around him, tacitly threatening the aliens. They stayed where they were, just staring.

Obviously he was aboard the ship he had seen in the woods. What could he do? The creatures seemed weak and disinclined to fight, yet what kind of defences might they have? They could be venomous or carry miniature versions of the ray that had struck him in the forest. Nevertheless, he had little choice. If he wanted to escape their examination, he had to attack. Walton had trained in karate and tensed himself, ready to strike.

As he did so, the creatures turned and fled the room. The surprise and relief was stunning and Walton almost collapsed. A second later, he realized that this might be his only opportunity to escape. Peering carefully out of the open door, Walton could see no sign of the aliens. There was just a dimly-lit curving corridor, about three feet wide, that ran past the door. Taking care to be quiet, Walton left the examination room and turned left down the corridor.

After about ten feet, Walton saw another open door on the left. He fought his impulse to just keep going until he found an escape route. This would probably be his only chance to learn more about an alien civilization. Swallowing his fear, he entered the room. It was circular, about 16 feet across, and rose to a domed ceiling. It was empty apart from a single high-backed chair standing at its center. The walls had the same brushed metal sheen as those of the examination room.

Walton stepped towards the chair. Instantly, the lights in the room dimmed. He jumped back in shock. The lights returned to their full strength. Stepping forwards again, Walton realised that the lighting was controlled by his proximity to the chair. Walking up to it, the lights faded to nothing and were replaced by tiny star-like points of light, glistening on the walls and ceiling. A grid was superimposed upon the "star," the lines of which were subdivided by smaller dashes.

By the soft light of the stars, Walton could see that there were some kind of controls built into the arms of the chair. Recklessly, he reached out and pressed a button-like protuberance. Around him, the lines of the grid slipped across each other, assuming a new position. Pulling a handle-like object, Walton succeeded in making the star-lights move downwards. He did not understand what was happening and clearly he was no nearer escape.

Walton stepped back from the chair, at a loss as to what to do. What if the stars on the wall represented what was outside the ship? He had recognized no constellations. He might be millions of miles from earth, with no means of returning. Just then, Walton heard a noise come from the open door. He spun around. Standing in the doorway was a tall male human being. He had blond hair and was wearing a blue suit with a black waist band. Over his head, he wore a bubble of transparent material. He gestured for Walton to come closer.

Here at last was something familiar, no matter how incongruous. Walton ran over to the man, babbling questions. The man did not reply but just smiled calmly. Walton decided that the helmet must stop his hearing. The man took Walton by the hand and led him back into the corridor.

They walked together to another, closed, door. As the man stopped in front of it, it slid open to reveal a small room. They stepped into it together and the door shut behind them. For two minutes they just stood silently, Walton too confused to ask any more questions. Then, a door opposite them slid open. Through it flowed bright light.

Walton followed the blue-suited man through the door and down a steep ramp. He found himself in a kind of hangar. The ramp that they had just descended led from the craft that he had seen in the forest. Around them sat other similar saucers, as well as two ovoid objects of about the same size with highly reflective surfaces. The ceiling of the hangar was patterned like a chess board with light shining from the white squares.

The man lead Walton to a door in the wall of the hangar, which opened onto a long hallway. As they walked down this, Walton saw closed sets of double doors on either side. They opened the set at the other end of the corridor and walked into a white room. Two more men and a woman were standing around a table. They were dressed in the same way as Walton's companion. Walton demanded to know what was happening. They did not answer. He was led to a chair and he sat down.

The three men stood around him. They reached down to take his elbows. Unsure about whether he should go with them, Walton did not stand willingly. The men carried him over to the table. Walton began to suspect that these people were not as friendly as he had hoped. The woman leant over him, holding a breathing mask. It had no pipe attached to it, only a black ball stuck to the back. As she held it over his nose and mouth, Walton lost consciousness.

Five days had passed since the UFO incident in the forest. Immediately after abandoning him to his fate, Walton's workmates had felt guilty and decided to go back and find him. As they stopped the truck, they had seen the golden saucer accelerate and disappear over the trees. They returned to the clearing. There was no sign of Walton. They began to wonder if they had the right place. As it was clear that they could not find him on their own, they decided to call the police.

Naturally the Arizona police were not impressed by the UFO story. However, there was no doubt that Walton had disappeared. A manhunt was quickly arranged, which combed the forest around the clearing for days. Nothing was found. As the days passed, it seemed increasingly unlikely that Travis Walton would be found alive. Yet how to explain his disappearance? The people who were last to see him alive were also the first to report that he had gone. It seemed extremely unlikely that they would murder Walton and then immediately ring the police. In order to establish some idea of what had happened, the Department of Public Safety asked the men if they would take a lie detector test. They agreed. After some initial anger at the gist of the questions in the test (most of which implied foul play), all the men were tested. According to the polygraph readings, they were not lying.

Then, around midnight on November 10, 1975, Travis Walton's brother-in-law, Grant Neff, received a phone call. At first he thought that it was a hoax and was about to hang up.

"Wait!" shouted the voice at the other end, "It's me Travis."

This time Grant recognized the voice. He asked "Travis" where he was. At the Exxon gas station in Heber, he was told. Still wary of a prank, Grant rang Travis's brother Duane and together they drove over to Heber to check if they were being hoaxed. When they arrived, they saw a figure huddled at the foot of the phone box. When the headlights of the truck shone on him, he looked up. It was Travis.

Immensely relieved that he was still alive, they bundled their stunned relative into the cab and set off for Travis's mother's house. As they drove, Travis tried to tell them what had happened to him. The words came in spurts, disordered and confused – big eyes, white skins, an hour aboard an alien ship. Clearly he did not know that he had been gone for five days. All that he remembered clearly was his arrival back on earth.

After falling unconscious in the white room, Travis had woken up lying on his stomach on what felt like tarmac. He felt cold, as though suddenly thrust from a warm room. Looking up, he saw the curved underside of the object from the forest. Silently, it rose and disappeared.

Looking around him, Walton had seen that he was lying by the side of the highway. It seemed to be just to the west of Heber, the town he had been heading for when he was abducted. He got up and ran, overwhelmingly relieved to be home. The first phone box he had tried had been out of order. It was from the second that he had called Grant, and it was there that Grant had found him.

Back at his mother's house, Travis stripped of his work clothes and examined himself. There were no marks on his body, save for a circular red blotch on his right elbow. Weighing himself, he found that he had lost ten pounds over the five days of his disappearance. He felt very hungry and thirsty and drank down pints of water. Eating, despite his hunger, made him feel sick. That night he was kept awake by nightmares.

On reporting to the police that he had returned, Travis was asked to take a polygraph test as his co-workers had. Despite his weak mental and physical state, Travis agreed. By the time that the test was to be performed, word of his return had leaked to the US tabloid press (who had been following the story closely since the disappearance.) Travis had also agreed to be examined by Dr James Harder, a member of a UFO monitoring group.

The polygraph test showed that Travis Walton believed that he had been abducted by aliens. This is made more remarkable by the fact that, at the time, Travis was suffering from great anxiety every time he tried to remember the abduction. This stress could easily have resulted in a false positive lie-detector result. Shortly afterwards, Dr Harder hypnotized Travis and asked him about his experiences. The facts in the above account are drawn from Travis's answers during this session.

Many people have accused Travis and his work colleagues of inventing the whole UFO story to get a little publicity and a little money. The most common skeptical explanation is that Travis hid in the woods for the five days and reappeared when the initial publicity caused by his "abduction" was beginning to flag. Indeed, an elderly couple claimed to have seen Travis hitchhiking on the highway during the period that he was supposed to be aboard the alien vessel.

If this version of events is the true one, then Travis and his co-conspirators certainly got what they were after. Travis wrote a book based upon his experiences called *The Walton Experience* in 1978. It sold well, was republished and expanded to coincide with the Paramount Pictures movie version of his story, "Fire In The Sky." In the latter version of the book, there is a full-page advert offering prints of paintings that depict scenes from the abduction priced at almost $400 each. A small industry has grown up around the incident, as tends to happen with all well-publicized UFO incidents. Yet, as with the Betty Andreasson abduction, the facts are so overwhelmingly strange that a hoax is difficult to credit.

> Terracotta figurines found in Ur in Southern Mesopotamia, seem to depict the creatures often described by UFO observers. The figures are thin, have bulbous foreheads and large almond-shaped eyes. The objects date from around 4500 BC.

Alien Brothers?

In nearly all cases of "alien" contact, the witnesses report that the extraterrestrials looked human. The "gray" (as it has come to be known by ufologists) is usually described as humanoid in shape and gray in complexion. Often they have large almond-shaped eyes. Over and over again, in unconnected close encounters, the same creatures have been reported. This has been used by UFO researchers as evidence that the aliens are a real extraterrestrial species.

It is worth pointing out here the immense chances against any extraterrestrial life resembling a human being. Our shape is dictated by evolutionary pressures. The idea that exactly the same pressures would be present on an alien planet is difficult to credit. Chimpanzees are over 99 per cent genetically identical to human beings. Yet they look less like us that the "grays" who are supposed to have evolved on another planet.

Almond Eyes

To counter this argument, it has been suggested that, for some unknown reason, life can only evolve one way into one basic shape. Of course, we do not have enough information to prove this to be true or false. Judging by the range of life on earth, it seems unlikely. So, are all cases of alien contact made up? The answer to this is certainly "no." There are too many cases and too much evidence for this to be possible. The fact that the creatures often seem to be humanoid only deepens the mystery . . . .

4

The Conspiracy

In 1955, Dr Morris K. Jessup, a Professor of astronomy and mathematics at the University of Michigan, published the first study of alien contact and possible human abduction. The book, The Case for the UFO, *argued that many mysterious disappearances might be attributable to UFOs. One of the cases he uses, cited from the writer R. Dewitt Miller (author of* Forgotten Mysteries*), has achieved a kind of classic status.*

"On September 23, 1880, David Lang – a farmer and prominent landowner living near Gallatin, Tennessee – returned home from a business trip. After greeting his family, he started walking across an 80 acre field to inspect his blooded horses.

"While he was walking across the field, his wife and two children saw a buggy approach along the road, and Lang stopped. In the buggy were Judge Peck, a local attorney, and a friend. When he saw Lang crossing the field, Peck stopped in his buggy and signalled the farmer to return to his house.

"There, in full view of five people – Lang's wife and two children, Peck and his friend – Lang vanished in a field which was devoid of trees, boulders, or any sort of cover; a field covered with grass and without caves, bogs, abandoned wells, or other chasms. In fact, a later geological survey showed this entire field was underlayed at a depth of a few feet with a solid stratum of limestone.

"The press of Tennessee was filled for months with stories about the 'Lang disappearance.' There were searches – made immediately following Lang's vanishing and for months afterwards.

"Bloodhounds were used. Detectives were called in. The story reached Vienna and a Doctor Hern stated, "There are vortices (in the so-called physical world) through which a man might vanish." Ambrose Bierce wrote a fictionalized version of the incident. The bloodhounds, the detectives and the theorists produce nothing.

"The case has been the subject of endless speculation. But no one has ever found a trace of David Lang. And there remains only the affidavit of Lang's daughter and the statements of the other witnesses that Lang simply vanished while crossing an open field."

Jessup concludes this section, "I submit that capture by a space contraption, for purposes beyond our ken, is the only truly satisfactory answer."

Regrettably, Jessup was incorrect. When I asked a friend in Tennessee to investigate the case, I discovered that a hardware salesman called Joe McHatten, having spent a boring day in Gallatin cofined to his room by snow, had whiled away the time by writing his wife a letter in which he had invented the whole story!

Soon after the publication of *The Case for the UFO*, Jessup received two letters from a man who signed himself Carlos Allende (or Carl Allen), who made an extraordinary claim – in October 1943, the US Navy had tried inducing a tremendously powerful magnetic field on board a destroyer in Philadelphia. As a result, the ship became completely invisible while sailors on board became semitransparent to one another's eyes. The ship itself vanished from its Philadelphia dock and reappeared at its other regular dock at Newport, Virginia. Half the crew, said Allende, became insane.

All this greatly excited Jessup because he had already formulated a similar theory about how UFOs can appear and disappear. He connected it with Einstein's "Unified Field Theory," which states, briefly, that "our compartmentalised concept of time-space and matter-energy are not separate entities but are transmutable under the same conditions of electromagnetic disturbance."

When he had been corresponding with Allende for some time, Jessup received an unexpected request to come to Washington by the Office of Naval Research (ONR), and was shown a copy of his own book with notes in three different handwritings. He thought he recognised one of these as that of Allende. Subsequently, the department of Naval Research had copies of the book duplicated, and apparently sent to various offices in the department.

Three years later, in April 1959, Jessup was found dead in his parked station-wagon in Dade County Park, Miami, with a hose connecting the exhaust to the interior of the car. Jessup's friend, Dr Manson Valentine, told Charles Berlitz (who reports it in his book *The Bermuda Triangle*), that Jessup had been approached by the Navy to continue working on the Philadelphia Experiment or similar projects, but had declined. Valentine admits that "some people" refused to believe that Jessup committed suicide and that there were "people or influences that wished to prevent" the spread of his theories.

And so, as early as the mid-1950s, the "conspiracy theories" had begun.

> Individuals who see UFOs are often visited subsequently by the "Men In Black" or MIBs. Claiming to be representatives of the government, these formally-dressed men resemble FBI officers or plainclothes policemen. They have been known to threaten witnesses if they reveal what they have seen. There are two main explanations offered for these visits. Some ufologists believe that the men work for a secret arm of government that knows that UFOs are real. Others argue that the MIBs are in fact aliens, disguised as government officials. It is hard to decide which is the more disturbing proposition . . . .

Project Blue Book

In September 1947, the US Air Force launched an investigation of UFOs, which was at that time code-named "Project Sign." In 1951, this became "Project Blue Book." It was located at the Wright Patterson Air Force Base in Dayton, Ohio, as part of the Air Technical Intelligence Center (ATIC), and later the Foreign Technology Division (FTD). For much of this time, "Project Blue Book" was under the direction of Dr Edward Condon of the University of Colorado. "Project Blue Book" was finally dropped by the Air Force in 1969 on Condon's recommendation – and after the publication of his Report.

In the late 1940s, the astronomer J. Allen Hynek was appointed astronomical consultant to the US Air Force and quickly became convinced that, whatever lay behind the UFO reports, they were undoubtedly not a hoax or a delusion.

Although a scientist himself, Hynek ended by being thoroughly critical of the attitude of scientists. He reports how, during an evening reception of several hundred astronomers in Victoria, British Columbia (in the summer of 1968), word spread through the hall that someone had seen manoeuvering lights outside. "The news was met by casual banter and the giggling sound that often accompanies an embarrassing situation. *Not one astronomer ventured outside in the summer night to see for himself* (My italics.)

The main value of Hynek's book *The UFO Experience: A Scientific Enquiry* (1972), is that it is so highly critical of the Air Force investigation and the Condon Report, which, as he says, gave the "kiss of death" to official UFO investigation. Condon had written, "while we do not think at present that anything is likely to come out of such research, each individual case ought to be carefully considered on its own merits" – which Hynek describes as "truly a masterpiece of throwing a scrap of meat to the critic dogs."

In fact, two members of Condon's team (David Saunders and Norman Levina) embarrassed Condon by publishing a memorandum written by the project coordinator, Robert Low, soon after it was initiated. This admitted, "our study would be conducted almost exclusively by nonbelievers who, although they couldn't possibly *prove* a negative result, could and probably would add an impressive body of evidence *that there is no reality to the observations*. (My italics.) The trick would be, I think, to describe the project so that to the public, it would appear a totally objective study, but to the scientific community, would present the image of a group of nonbelievers trying their best to be objective, but having an almost zero expectation of finding a saucer." It goes on to recommend that the emphasis should be put on the psychology of the kind of people who report UFOs – in other words, suggests that these are nuts and cranks. When this was published, Condon was furious and dismissed Saunders and Levina for insubordination. The result, of course, is that most serious students of the UFO phenomenon take a skeptical and negative view of officialdom and its opinions.

This kind of skepticism seems to have been justified by the reaction to a flurry of UFO sightings in and around Exeter, New Hampshire, in the autumn of 1965. A Mrs Jalbert, with her four sons, saw a silvery object with bright flashing lights hovering near power lines near their home – occasionally an aircraft would pursue it. Two young people saw a UFO emerge from the sea at Hampton Beach which then pursued their car. A Mrs Bloggett saw a blinding ball of light rotating at high speed over the treetops. And at around 1.30 a.m. on September 3, 1965, a patrolman named Bertrand checked a parked car and was told by the distraught woman inside it that she had been followed for 12 miles by a huge, silent UFO, which had flown off at great speed. When he got back to the Police Station, the patrolman found an 18-year-old boy called Norman Muscarello, who declared that he had also seen a giant, silent UFO when he was hitch-hiking to his home in Exeter. He said that it was bigger than a house and appeared to be 80 or 90 feet in diameter, with brilliant, pulsating red lights around an apparent rim. He dived into a ditch and the object moved away – after which he quickly hitched a lift into Exeter.

Muscarello and Patrolman Bertrand hurried back to the spot, where they found "a group of five red lights . . . . extremely bright (which) flashed on one at a time. The lights started to move around over the field. At one time, they came so close I fell to the ground and started to draw my gun . . . . there was no sound or vibration but the farm animals were upset and making a lot of noise . . . . I radioed Patrolman David Hunt, who arrived in a few minutes. He also observed the lights . . . ."

But when all this was reported, investigators from Pease Air Force Base pointed out that five B-47 Bombers were airborne at the time of the sightings. Then, on October 27, the Pentagon issued a statement saying that the sightings were due to aircraft taking part in a Strategic Air Command exercise, and to distortions of stars and planets caused by the high temperature. A month later, the police had an unsolicited letter from "Project Blue Book" suggesting that the sightings had been caused by a high altitude Air Force exercise. When the officers pointed out that this had ended at 2.00 a.m., the Pentagon's response was to reclassify the sightings as "unknown."

A journalist named John G. Fuller became interested in the sightings and went himself to investigate. He actually saw a bright orange-red disc being pursued by a jet fighter. All this seemed to indicate that the Air Force knew something about what was going on – a conclusion Fuller goes to some length to emphasize in his best selling book *Incident at Exeter* (1966). Another expert on UFOs, Major Donald E. Keyhoe, expressed the same kind of doubts in a book called *Aliens From Space* (1973).

On Tuesday, November 9, 1965, an enormous black-out on the east coast of America plunged 80,000 square miles into darkness – 36 million people – one fifth of America's population – were affected. Nearly 800,000 people were trapped for hours in elevators and under-ground trains while airline pilots circled trying to find a way to land at darkened airports. Fortunately, few people seem to have been injured or even seriously inconve-nienced, although nine months later, statisticians noted a surge in the birth rate which indicated that most Americans had chosen a predictable alternative to tele-vision.

Two days later, it was announced that the problem had been caused by a break in the power line from Niagara. A check showed that this was untrue. Then the authorities announced that the problem lay at a remote-control sub-station at Clay, New York, where high tension wires above the town are part of a "super highway" of power from Niagara Falls to New York City. But repair men who drove out to Clay found nothing wrong.

In *Incident at Exeter*, John Fuller reports, "something else happened outside Syracuse, however, which was noted briefly in the press, and then immediately dropped without follow-up comment. Weldon Ross, a private pilot and instructor, was approaching Hancock Field at Syracuse for a landing. It was at almost the exact moment of the blackout. As he looked below him, just over the power lines near the Clay sub-station, a huge red ball of brilliant intensity appeared. It was about a hundred feet in diameter, Ross told the New York *Journal-American*. He calculated that the fireball was at the point where the New York Power Authority's two

345,000-volt power-lines at the Clay sub-station pass over New York Central's tracks between Lake Oneida and Hancock Field. With Ross was a student pilot who verified the statement. At precisely the same moment, Robert C. Walsh, Deputy Commissioner for the Federal Aviation Agency in the Syracuse area, reported that he saw the same phenomenon just a few miles south of Hancock Field. A total of five people reported the sighting. Although the Federal Power Commission immediately said they would investigate, no further word has been given publicly since."

Major Donald Keyhoe continues the story, "other pilots and assorted witnesses reported other sightings elsewhere. Two civilians in flight over Pennsylvania shortly before the blackout began witnessed two UFOs flying above them with Air Force jet interceptors in pursuit. Also, just before the blackout began, a UFO was sighted near the Niagara Falls Power Plant. After it was all over, experts investigating the cause of the breakdown traced its origin to the area of the Clay sub-station, but were unable to find anything wrong with the equipment. When the investigators and journalists began to take the hypothesis of UFO intervention seriously, a previously overlooked broken relay in Ontario was announced to be the cause of the disaster. However, later investigation brought out that the supposedly broken relay had in fact never broken. The supposedly infallible billion dollar US-Canadian grid system dissolved in four seconds flat as the network was suddenly and simultaneously drained of power in some sectors while being overloaded in others. The multiple safety controls supposed to be effective in such an emergency did not work at all. They had worked effectively during previous smaller scale emergency situations. In 1968, Congressman William F. Ryan put McDonald on record concerning UFO activity at the time of the great power failure. Dr McDonald charged the Federal Power Commission with evading the evidence connecting UFOs to the power failure. As Dr McDonald made this accusation in Congress, it was entered in the Congressional Record."

McDonald's statements provoked a torrent of abuse and violent criticism from his colleagues, who denounced him as a crank. On June 13, 1971, McDonald was found dead, shot through the head with a pistol by his side. The official verdict was suicide.

Again, we note the witnesses who saw UFOs being pursued by aeroplanes, with the implication that the Air Force knew beyond all doubt of the real existence of UFOs, and that the announcement in the Condon Report (four years later), that UFOs constituted no threat to national security, may well have been guided by a desire to prevent widespread panic.

The case of Frank Edwards, the journalist who wrote best selling books with titles like *Strange People* and *Strange World*, has often been cited as someone who was deliberately "silenced." In the 1960s, Edwards ran an extremely popular radio show sponsored by the American Federation of Labor. But he became fascinated by the subject of flying saucers and wrote a book called *Flying Saucers – Serious Business*, on whose fly leaf appeared a warning that stated that flying saucers can be harmful to human beings, warning readers not to attempt to touch a UFO that has landed. It became a bestseller; but Edwards lost his job on the radio station. George Meany, president of the American Federation of

Labor, admitted that Edwards had been dropped "because he talked too much about flying saucers." Edwards learned later that his mention of flying saucers had irritated the Defence Department who had brought pressure to bear on Meany.

Edwards was not silenced for long – he soon had his own syndicated radio show that dealt almost exclusively with flying saucers. But in June 1967, whilst still in his 50s, Edwards collapsed and died. The news of his death caused consternation at the 1967 Congress of Scientific Ufologists in New York's Hotel Commodore, because it so happened that the day, June 24, was precisely 20 years after Kenneth Arnold had made the first well-known UFO sighting near Mount Rainier. Edwards's obituary stated that his death was "apparently due to a heart attack." But whether his death has some genuine sinister connotation, there can be no doubt that he was, in fact, silenced for a while by the US Defence Department.

Was Edwards merely being paranoid in believing that UFOs can be dangerous? Ufologist Jacques Vallee has argued strongly that this is untrue. In a book called *Confrontations* (1990), he cites many cases in which it seems that human beings have been physically damaged – sometimes killed – by their contact with UFOs. In 1980, Vallee and his wife Janine went to investigate a case that had taken place near Rio de Janeiro in August 1966. An 18-year-old boy had found the corpses of two men when he was looking for a lost kite. They were dressed in neat suits and new raincoats and lying on their backs. There was no blood, no sign of violence at the site. The two corpses were lying peacefully side by side. Next to them were crude metal masks and slips of paper covered with notes. One of these notes contained elementary electrical formulae.

The corpses were decomposed and the coroner concluded that death was caused by cardiac arrest – although he did not explain why two men had died of it at the same time. He was able to say that the men had died some time between August 16 and August 20. The men were identified as electronics technicians named Miguel Jose Viana (34), and Manuel Pereira da Cruz (32). Both lived in the town of Campos and specialized in putting up local TV transmitters.

When news of the double death was publicised, a society woman named Gracinda de Souza reported that she had been driving with three of her children on Wednesday, August 17, when they saw an oval object, orange in color, with a line of fire around its edges "sending out rays in all directions". It hovered over the hill where the bodies were found. Soon after this, many witnesses called the police to report that they had seen an orange-colored, egg-shaped object giving off blue rays over the hill.

The metal masks – they were actually made of lead – naturally gave rise to a suspician that the men were expecting to encounter something that might give off dangerous rays.

Jacques Vallee became interested in the case when a doctor named Olavo Fontes visited him in Chicago in 1967 and handed him a bundle of reports which included an account of the strange deaths. It also mentioned an event that had taken place a few months before the sighting, on March 16, 1966, when a luminous object, eliptical in shape, was seen at an altitude of 100 feet not far from the later sightings.

When Vallee and his wife went to Brazil in 1980 to

investigate the site of the tragedy, he began to gather information about other people who had been seriously damaged by UFOs. He learned, for example, of an event that had taken place in 1946, when two men, Prestes Filho and a friend, were returning from a fishing trip near the village of Aracriguama and who separated at 7.00 p.m. An hour later, Prestes staggered into his sister's home with a story of a beam of light that had hit him as he was reaching his front door. That same evening, his condition deteriorated and Vallee learned that "his flesh literally detached itself from his bones. It was as if he had been boiled in hot water for a long time, so that his skin and the underlying tissue fell." On route to the hospital, he died. Later, the skin continued to fall away from his body until his corpse looked "decomposed." The possibility that he was struck by lightning was discounted when it was revealed that on the evening in question the sky was perfectly clear.

On August 17, 1962, in the town of Duas Pontes, Brazil, a man called Rivalino Mafra noticed two small beings digging a hole near his house – they ran away as he came closer and moments later he saw an object shaped like a hat take off from behind some bushes, surrounded by a red glow. On August 19 (two days later), Rivalino and his three sons were awakened by the sound of heavy footsteps and saw shadows shaped like human beings floating through the house and voices that threatened them. One of the sons later testified to the police, "I saw two balls floating in mid air side by side, about a foot apart, and three feet off the ground . . . . they were big . . . . one of them was black, with a kind of irregular antenna-like extension and a small tail. The other was black and white with the same outline . . . .

both emitted a humming sound . . . . I called my father out of the house . . . . he walked towards the object and stopped about two yards away. At that moment the two big spheres merged into each other. There was now only one, bigger in size, raising dust from the ground, and giving off smoke that darkened the sky. With strange sounds, the large ball crept slowly towards my father.

"I saw him surrounded by yellow smoke; he disappeared inside it. I ran after him into the yellow cloud, which had an acrid smell. I saw nothing, only that yellow mist around me. I yelled for my father but there was no answer. Everything was silent again. Then the yellow smoke dissolved. The spheres were gone. My father was gone . . . . I want my father back." A local doctor called Pereira had also seen a disc-shaped object on the day of Rivalino's disappearance.

Vallee also reports a case that took place on July 5, 1969, near the town of Anolaima, Colombia, about 40 miles northwest of Bogota. At 8.30 p.m., two children saw a luminous object 300 yards away. They grabbed a flashlight and sent out signals. It came closer and the children called out the rest of the family, and all 13 people who lived in the farmhouse watched the light as it flew off and disappeared behind a hill. The father, 54-year-old Arcesio Bermudez, took the flashlight and went to investigate. When he came back he was frightened. From a distance of less than 20 feet he had seen a small person inside the top part of the object, which was transparent, while the rest of the craft was dark. He saw this being when he turned on his flashlight. The object then became bright and took off.

Over the next few days his health deteriorated and 48 hours after the sighting he felt sick. He was unable to eat, and had dark blue spots on his skin. Seven days later he died. But the doctors who diagnosed gastroenteritis as the cause of death were not told about the UFO incident, and one of them later commented, "if I had known of his experience I would have performed more tests."

In one incident described by Vallee, five people died near the town of Panorama at different times, following close encounters with UFOs. These were all deer-hunters, who had climbed into trees at night to wait for their quarry. Witnesses reported rectangular objects sometimes looking like refrigerators, flying over the treetops and shining a beam towards the earth – local inhabitants came to call them "chupas." Rivamar Ferreira was out with his friend, Abel Boro, on October 17, 1981, when they saw a light that turned night into day. Abel screamed as the object – looking like a giant spinning truck tyre with lights on it – surrounded his body with a glittering glow. Ferreira ran to Abel's house and returned with his family – they found Abel Boro dead, his body white "as if drained of blood."

During the preliminary stages of NASA's "Gemini" program, unmanned capsules were fired into earth's orbit to test rocket technology. On April 18, 1964, radar monitoring the first of these capsules picked up a formation of four other objects, closely following the capsule. They remained in formation with the capsule during an entire orbit, after which they peeled away in an orderly fashion and flew out of the radar's range.

In another case, a man called Dionizio General was on top of a hill when an object hovered over him and shot a beam at him like "a big ray of fire." A witness testified that he seemed to receive a shock and came rolling down the hill. For the next three days he was insane with terror, then died. Vallee also cites cases in which two victims, Raimundo Souza, and a man named Ramon who lived in Panorama, died shortly after similar encounters.

Interviewing local inhabitants of Panorama, Vallee noted that one witness compared the beam to an electric arc, while another said he remembered a very bad smell like an electrical odor and saw a blinding light, with pulsating colors inside. Many other people who reported being exposed to "chupas" as they were lying in tree hammocks said that, several years later, they still suffered from headaches and general weakness, and had lost their previous vitality.

Jacques Vallee concludes his chapter with the comment, "many of the injuries described in Brazil . . . . are consistent with the effects of high-power pulsed microwaves." In other words, there is a sense in which the victims were "cooked" exactly as if they had placed their hands in an unprotected microwave oven.

The ufologist, John Keel, is convinced that the "visitors from space" have other ways of destroying people. In *Operation Trojan Horse* he tells a strange story.

In 1959, there appeared a typical "contactee" book called *My Contact With Flying Saucers* by a man who called himself Dino Craspedon, written originally in Portuguese. The author claims that, in November 1952, he was touring with a friend in the States of Sao Paolo and that on reaching the top of the Angatuba Range, they saw five flying saucers hovering in the air. He went back to the same spot later and spent three days and nights in the hope of seeing a saucer again. On the last night, he claims that a saucer landed and he was taken inside it by the captain and introduced to its crew.

In March 1953, there was a knock at Dino Craspedon's door – his name was actually Aladino Felix – and a man who looked like a parson asked if he could speak to Aladino. To Aladino's surprise, it was the captain from a flying saucer. Aladino claims that the captain revealed himself to be a man of tremendous erudition, speaking Greek, Latin and Hebrew, and claiming that he came from a satellite of Jupiter.

The book that followed was basically a dialogue between Aladino and the captain of the spacecraft. It differs from most "contactee" books in being full of rather precise scientific detail and even a certain amount of mathematics. The book failed to cause any sensation at the time and most people naturally dismissed it as fiction – like the works of George Adamski. However, John Keel seems to feel that the book is genuine. He says, "a careful reading reveals a thorough knowledge of both theology and science, and many of the ideas and phrases found only in most obscure occult and contactee literature appear here. Among other things, the book also discusses an impending cosmic disaster in lucid almost convincing terms; the same kind of warning that is passed on to every contactee in one way or another."

Keel goes on to explain that in 1965, Aladino Felix turned up in Brazil claiming to be able to predict the future. He warned of a disaster about to take place in Rio de Janeiro, and a month later, floods and landslides killed 600 people. In 1966, he warned that a Russian cosmonaut would die, and in April 1967, Vladimir

Komarov became the first man to die in space. In the autumn of 1967, Felix appeared on television in Brazil to soberly discuss the forthcoming assassinations in the United States of Martin Luther King and Senator Robert Kennedy. When he started predicting an outbreak of bombings and murders in Brazil, in 1968, no one was greatly surprised when a wave of terrorist attacks began. "Police stations and public buildings in Sao Paolo were dynamited. There was a wave of bank robberies, and an armored payroll train was heisted. The Brazilian police worked overtime and soon rounded up 18 members of the gang. A 25 year-old policeman named Jesse Morais proved to be the gang's bomb expert. They had blown up Second Army Headquarters, a major newspaper, and even the American Consulate. When the gang members started to sing, it was learned that they planned to assassinate top government officials and eventually take over the entire country of Brazil. Jesse Morais had been promised the job of Police Chief in the new government.

"The leader of this ring was . . . . Aladino Felix!

"When he was arrested on August 22, 1968, the flying saucer prophet declared, 'I was sent here as an ambassador to the earth from Venus. My friends from space will come here and free me and avenge my arrest. You can look for tragic consequences to humanity when the flying saucers invade this planet'."

Keel comments, "once again the classic, *proven* pattern has occurred. Another human being had been engulfed by the ultraterrestrials and led down the road to ruin. There is no clinical psychiatric explanation for these cases. These men (and it has happened to women too), experienced a succession of convincing events with flying saucers and the UTs. Then they were smothered with promises or ideas which destroyed them."

If Keel is correct, then the "space people" themselves seem as anxious to cover-up their activities as the government agencies denounced by Hynek and Vallee.

The "Majestic 12" documents

In 1987, UFO investigator William L. Moore received a cartridge of photographic film in the mail. Naturally curious about its contents, he had it developed. What he found looked like the answer to every Ufologist's prayers. Each exposure was a page from a document. The first was headed, "BRIEFING DOCUMENT: OPERATION MAJESTIC 12 PREPARED FOR PRESIDENT-ELECT DWIGHT D. EISENHOWER NOVEMBER 18, 1952." Astonishingly, it seemed to be an account of the UFO phenomenon from inside the government, drawn up to explain extraordinary secrets to the incoming president.

The "briefing" began by giving the names of 12 government officials all drawn from the scientific and intelligence communities. Together they formed a secret committee known as "Majestic 12" (or MJ-12). Apparently, it was this committee's responsibility to investigate UFO sightings and wreckage, while the more public "Project Blue Book" provided a cover, by writing off UFOs as imaginary or as natural phenomena.

The document went on to give a detailed description of the Roswell incident of July 1947. It told of four alien bodies that had been recovered from an area two miles east of the Roswell crash site. They were all dead and badly mutilated by desert predators. The committee had concluded that the alien pilots had ejected from their ship before it crashed.

According to the document, General Nathan F. Twining and Dr Vannevar Bush, both committee members, had analyzed the wreckage. Noting that it was small and seemed to have had no provisions on board, they came to the conclusion that it was a short-range reconnaissance vehicle. As to the technology that had made it, there seemed to be nothing that the scientists could identify as jets, wings or engines of any kind. In addition, there was no wiring or electronics as understood by terrestrial science. The committee decided that whatever the propulsion was, it had been totally destroyed in the crash.

A Dr Detlev Bronk was said to have performed the analysis of the four dead aliens. They were humanoid in appearance, yet the structure of their bodies suggested that they had evolved in a way very different to Homo sapiens. The document called the aliens E.B.Es (standing for Extraterrestrial Biological Entities.)

The next question that the "Majestic 12" committee turned to was the location of the alien's home world. Mars was put forward as a possibility. Dr Donald Menzel suggested that they came from another planetary system entirely.

According to the briefing, some writing was found on the Roswell craft. All attempts to decipher it had failed.

The document concludes, "Implications for the National Security are of continuing importance in that the motives and ultimate intentions of these visitors remain completely unknown. In addition, a significant upsurge in the surveillance activity of these craft beginning in May and continuing through the autumn of this year has caused considerable concern that new developments may be imminent. It is for these reasons as well as the obvious international and technological considerations and the ultimate need to avoid a public panic at all costs that the "Majestic 12" group remains of the unanimous opinion that the imposition of the strictest security precautions should continue without interruption into the new administration."

Timothy Good, in his book *Alien Contact*, quotes from documents said to be secret government briefings drawn up during the administration of President Carter, in the late 1970s. Here is one of the excerpts:

"In late 1949, another alien aircraft crashed in the United States and was recovered partly intact by the military. One alien survived the crash . . . . the alien's language was translated by means of picturegraphs. It was learned that the alien came from a planet in the "Zeta Reticula" star system . . . . [The alien] lived until June 18, 1952, when he died of an unexplained illness."

Rumors of such alien contacts abound in the ufological community. Although many investigators claim to have learnt about the contacts through leaks from the US intelligence services, nothing resembling convincing proof has ever surfaced.

This was the "smoking gun" that UFO researchers had been looking for. It answered all the questions. It confirmed the conspiracy theory. It confirmed that "Project Blue Book" had been a front for real, top secret investigations going on at the heart of government. It confirmed that the Roswell incident had not been caused by a crashed weather balloon. Could such an important document have been leaked?

Understandably, many investigators thought that it was too good to be true. At the same time many stood by it as vindication of what they had been saying all along. With these battle-lines drawn, the serious analysis of the document began. The debunkers started by pointing out that the date format used in the "Majestic 12" briefing was not that used by the military at the time it was supposed to have been written. The document gave the date of the Roswell incident as "07 July, 1947". Research showed that the comma and the leading zero were not normally used.

Stan Friedman, a researcher who believed the document to be genuine, set about finding other military documents from the early '50s to see if any of them used this date format. While he did find many that featured an extra comma, the zero proved to be unique. It was obvious that the date neither confirmed nor denied the briefing's validity.

Skeptics soon found more to criticise. The document was supposed to have been written by Rear Admiral Roscoe H. Hillenkoetter, who was to go on to be the first head of the CIA, when it was formed later that year. In the document, his name is given as Admiral Roscoe H. Hillenkoetter. While the omission of the "Rear" from Hillenkoetter's title may seem a small issue, it cast more doubt on the briefing. Proponents argued that Hillenkoetter would in fact have been known as "Admiral." It was common military practise to leave out the prefix when speaking. Yet this was a written document, and if it was written by Hillenkoetter, he was effectively promoting himself by a rank when writing to the President – something that was hard to credit.

Then there were the numerous misspellings such as "boder" for "border" and "liason" for "liaison." Again, in a document intended for the President they were difficult to explain.

Included on the roll of film given to Moore was the image of a memo, supposedly signed by President Truman on September 24, 1947. It provided the authorization for the "Majestic 12" committee to fulfil their role, investigating the UFO threat in secret. Not surprisingly, this too was attacked as a forgery. Its format was wrong, the skeptics argued. It contained a salutation ("Dear Secretary Forrestal"), which was not normal for memos at the time. There were also problems with the signature. President Truman normally crossed into the printed area of his letters and memos with the flamboyant "T" of his signature. On the "Majestic 12" memo it was well clear of the text. Careful examination of other letters signed by Truman revealed that the signature on the memo was extremely similar to another signature on a letter to Dr Vannevar Bush. Proponents of the briefing cited this as evidence that it was real, critics said that it had been traced from the Bush letter.

Researchers tried to trace the executive order number on the Truman memo. Each order given by the president is numbered for the benefit of future historians. The number given on the "MJ-12" memo did not fit in with the sequence used at that period. In fact, the memo's executive order number was 092447, which was in fact the date on which it was supposed to have been written – September 24, 1947. Naturally, those who believed that

Harry Truman

the document was real pointed out that this was no ordinary order, and it would have been surprising if it *were* numbered as part of the sequence.

Nevertheless, the evidence was mounting up against the "MJ-12" briefing. Just as the ufological community was coming to the conclusion that it was a fake, Moore came up with another interesting find. This time, he found it in a recently declassified bundle of government documents.

Searching through Record Group 341 at the National Archive, Moore had come across a memo sent to General Twining, an officer named in the "MJ-12" document. Sent on July 14, 1954, the memo was from Robert Cutler, President Eisenhower's special assistant. It requested the rescheduling of a meeting of the "Majestic 12" committee. Just when it was needed, a document had emerged that gave external support to the "MJ-12" briefing's faltering credibility. The fact that it was General Twining who had provided this support was ironic.

Another letter of General Twining's had been used as evidence in the UFO argument for years. In it, Twining refers to the "lack of physical evidence in the shape of crash-recovered exhibits which would undeniably prove the existence of [UFOs]." The letter was written only two months after the Roswell incident, in September 1947. Now, it seemed, the Ufologists had proof of what they had suspected all along, that Twining's 1947 letter was just another instance of the cover-up.

Not to be deterred, the skeptics set to work on the new Twining memo. First they pointed out that its security classification – "Top Secret Restricted" – was in fact two separate classifications joined together. Others pointed out that the box in which Moore had found the memo had just been subjected to a security review to see if it could be declassified. If the Twining-Cutler memo had been found in the box, it would have been handed back to the National Security Council, whose responsibility it was. Even if they had decided to declassify it, it would not have been in Record Group 341.

Despite what some would consider to be damning evidence against the "Majestic 12" documents, they remain an active part of UFO folklore. Like the Roswell autopsy film, the will to believe in the events they describe carries any "evidence" along with it. As there is no solid chain of custody for the documents, it is not difficult to believe that Moore faked the "MJ-12" briefing and the Truman memo, and planted the faked Twining-Cutler memo in the National Archive.

Moore has since said that he knows that Twining has worked closely with representatives of the US government in the past. Like many Ufologists, he argues that the government deliberately passes out documents and other information that confirms their knowledge of UFOs. Combined with this, they distribute obvious lies and disinformation. In this way, the theory goes, they hope to discredit those who get uncomfortably close to the truth, while hiding the facts where they are safest – in plain view of the public.

5

Cattle Cutters and Crop Circles

In September 1967, near Alamosa in the San Luis Valley, Colorado, an Apaloosa mare named Lady was found dead and mutilated. Both her head and neck were completely stripped of their flesh. In the nights leading up to the discovery, strange lights had been seen in the sky above the valley. In fact, San Luis Valley had gained a reputation for strange lights. They had been appearing all that summer.

On the morning after Lady's discovery, Dr John Altshuler had driven up to the valley to see if he could see any of the strange lights for himself. As he stood by his car staring at the sky, a park ranger approached him and asked if he could examine the mutilated horse that they had just found. Altshuler was a doctor of pathology and had no experience of dead animals. Nevertheless he agreed.

Despite his lack of experience, it was obvious to Altshuler that the animal had not been killed by predators. As well as the complete removal of the head flesh, the horse had had its chest cut open and its internal organs removed. None of the animal's wounds bled and there were no signs of blood on the ground around it. The edges of the wounds seemed to have been sealed closed by a great heat. Altshuler took some tissue specimens from around the cuts and took them back to his hospital lab for analysis. Meanwhile Lady's owner, Berle Lewis, began searching the field for clues. The only tracks he could find belonged to the horse. Weirdly, these stopped about 100 feet from where Lady had been found. It was as though she had been picked up and dropped. Looking further, Lewis found a three-foot circle of holes in the earth, about 40 feet from the corpse. Close to the circle was a bush that had been burnt.

When Dr Altshuler examined his samples under the microscope, he found what he had expected. Along the edge of the cuts, the haemoglobin of the animal's blood had been cooked solid. This explained why there was no bleeding – wounds had been cauterized. No one was ever prosecuted for the attack. If it had been the only case of its kind, it would probably have been forgotten. But it was not the only case.

No official figures are available for the number of US mutilations, but few would dispute that over the course of the 1970s, it rose into the thousands. Between the years 1975 and 1977, two counties in Colorado alone suffered over 200 attacks. Mutilations have been recorded in the US, South America, Europe, Australia and Japan. Taken in isolation, each case could be put down to an attack by a violent madman. Yet this would not explain the many similarities between cases.

A case from Meeker County, Minnesota, in 1974, is typical. The victim was a heifer. Cattle are the most common victims of mutilation. Its eyes, cheek, left ear and tongue had been removed. The field in which it was found was covered with a scattering of snow. There were

112

no tracks to be seen. The only disturbances were circles of melted snow, one of which surrounded the dead cow. Other circles were scattered at random around the field. As with Lady, the wounds were bloodless and cauterized. There was no blood on the ground. The removal of the cheek and eye is extremely common. Many cattle also have other areas of skin removed. Usually the cut that separates the skin does not cut the muscle beneath. This, combined with the cauterization of the wounds, seems to point to a careful surgical operation rather than a frenzied attack.

Other types of mutilation are seen again and again. The entire anus and a tube of flesh around it is often cored out, leaving a bloodless hole under the tail. Sometimes the genitals of female animals are removed in this way as well. Udders and penises are cut off by slicing out a circle of surrounding skin. The edges of these wounds are often not only cauterized but serrated, as though cut with red-hot pinking shears.

These similarities, combined with the odd nature of the wounds, seem to point to an organized group of mutilators. When the attacks began to become widespread in the early 1970s, Vietnam veterans were put forward as possible culprits. Throughout the war, stories had come back to America about US troops torturing prisoners and cutting trophies from the bodies of fallen Vietcong soldiers. The suspicion was that the battle-hardened soldiers had gained a taste for mutilation and were practising it on animals. No serious evidence has ever been found to support this argument.

In 1980, television journalist Linda Moulton Howe produced a documentary on the mutilations called "A Strange Harvest." Showing many photographs of dead animals, the program covered the strange uniformity of the attacks. Shortly after the program was shown, the Royal Canadian Mounted Police contacted the producer. They were disturbed by the similarities between the cases covered in the film and a series of animal mutilations that they were investigating. The film had pointed out that many mutilated cattle had a section of tooth and bone cut from their lower jaw. This was also true of the Canadian cases. The Mounted Police had not released this information to the press. This was to help them tell the difference between the work of the original criminal and other "copy cat" crimes.

In the case of the Canadian mutilations, the Mounted Police had come to the conclusion that some kind of Satanic cult was attacking the animals as part of their rituals. The cases were too similar and too neat to be the work of separate deranged mutilators. Linda Moulton Howe's film contained details of attacks in the US that matched the Canadian cases exactly. The Mounted Police were faced with only two possibilities. Perhaps the attacks were all committed by different people, despite their similarities. The only other alternative was that the "Satanic cult" extended all over North America, and involved hundreds if not thousands of people.

No one, in the US or Canada, has ever been prosecuted for the attacks. In the US, an investigation that covered all of the cases could only be made by the FBI. Some of the mutilations have taken place on Indian Reserves, which puts them directly under FBI jurisdiction. Yet there has never been a Federal government investigation . . . .

Killers From The Sky?

During the spring of 1975, Texas suffered its worst spate of cattle mutilations. Over the same period, many Texans were reporting unmarked helicopters flying illegally low over herds of livestock. A complaint was filed with the Federal Aviation Authority. The FAA looked into the sightings, quizzing the local military bases and air contractors and announced that they did not know who was responsible.

Later that year, exactly the same phenomenon was disturbing farmers in northern New Mexico. The FAA announced in the local newspapers that an investigation was being started. Then nothing more was heard about it. When angry farmers later tried to force the information out of the FAA (using the Freedom of Information laws), they denied ever having made the investigation.

What is the link between the mysterious helicopters and cattle mutilation? Researcher Tom Adams has recorded over 200 cases in which unidentified helicopters have been seen buzzing over mutilation sites. They are seen both before and after the attacks. It is easy to see how a helicopter could be useful to a potential mutilator. Investigators have often theorized that the mutilations could not have happened where the bodies were found. Despite the cauterization of the wounds, it would be impossible not to make some mess when pulling organs from a cow's stomach. If the animals were taken somewhere else to be cut up, it would explain the lack of blood at the scene. It would also explain how Lady came to be 100 feet from her last track, and why so many mutilations are found with no footprints of any kind around them. Others have pointed out that the cauterized wounds are very similar to those made by a surgical laser. At the moment, such devices are nowhere near being portable. Some kind of transport would be needed to get them to the scene of the mutilations.

The connection drawn between unmarked helicopter sightings and cattle mutilations suggests to many a mysterious but terrestrial organisation. Some have even accused the US government of being behind the attacks. Any such organisation would have to put great resources into committing what is really a very petty crime. It is hard to imagine a situation in which they would not just buy cattle of their own and torture them in private. Even a Satanic cult would probably raise their own sacrifices.

The helicopter sightings do not necessarily suggest a terrestrial culprit however. In 1978, David Rees (a British UFO investigator) interviewed a Kent housewife called Mrs Clark about her experience of a phantom helicopter. While out gardening, Mrs Clark had looked up to see a helicopter hovering only feet above her. She saw two men in the cockpit, one looking down at her while the other looked ahead. She was so startled that she fell over as she tried to duck. All the time staring at the pilot, Mrs Clark got up and ran into the house. When her husband came home, she told him about the strange helicopter. He asked if it had blown the washing about the garden, or deafened her with the roar of its engines. David Rees goes on to quote Mrs Clark, "It was only then that I realized that there must have been something strange about it, for when he was asking these questions, I realized that there had been no sound and no downdrafts from the rotors, which I had not noticed at the time. The two men looked like ordinary beings and so did the helicopter. The window of the 'copter was all-in-one and I did not notice any landing gear or wheels. No markings at all.''

Was Mrs Clark hallucinating? Many mysterious helicopter sightings feature the same, seemingly impossible assertion. Helicopters make a deafening noise, yet these mysterious vehicles seem to be as silent as gliders. Could the helicopters be just an image, a disguise projected by extraterrestrials to hide their craft?

Lady, the first recorded victim of the mysterious mutilations, was attacked in San Luis Valley, Colorado, a place still known today for its frequent UFO sightings. Again and again, mysterious lights have been seen in the area of cattle mutilations. As with helicopters, there is a large body of circumstantial evidence linking more traditional UFOs with the mutilation phenomenon.

During 1993, Alabama began to experience a rash of cattle mutilations. Alabama has a history of UFO sightings and animal attacks. The last cluster of weird happenings had been in 1989. Four years later, it looked like the visitors were back. The first people to see a UFO in the 1993 wave were the Fyffe Police Chief and his assistant, out on a call in early January. They reported a huge triangular craft, twinkling with red, green and blue lights, gliding through the night sky approximately, 1,500 feet above their patrol car. Another very credible witness, this time a Baptist minister, had a terrifying experience with a UFO shortly afterwards.

Pastor Roger Watkins and his family were woken at 2.00 a.m. by a roaring sound. Their house in Geraldine, Alabama, was shaking so hard that they were afraid it would rip apart. At first, they thought they were in a hurricane. The Pastor's teenage son, Chris Watkins, ran

117

to his upstairs bedroom window to see what was going on. Outside, he saw a massive rounded disc, lit underneath by pulsing multicolored lights, hovering about six feet from the ground. The object was only 50 feet from the house, just outside their fence. The Pastor himself was also watching the disc from his downstairs bedroom window. Using the fence posts as a guide, he estimated that it was about 150 feet across. The Pastor and his son stood watching the object from their respective windows, shouting to each other in amazement. After about ten minutes, the disc began to spin and rose up into the sky. Soon it had disappeared.

Too terrified to sleep, the Pastor began to assess the damage to his house. His goldfish had been shaken from their bowls by the vibration. Obviously this had not been a hallucination – "I don't know what we saw, but I know it was real, it shook those fish out of the bowls, and it didn't look like anything I've ever seen on this earth before." Throughout the year, similar sightings to this, as well as the more usual dancing lights in the sky, were reported all over Alabama. Coinciding exactly with the wave of UFO sightings, animal mutilations began to be found.

Just after the Fyffe Police Chief saw his massive triangular UFO, on January 9, 1993, the Chief of Detectives for Albertsville found one of his cattle dead. Its stomach had been slit open and some internal organs pulled out. Tissue from the animal's rectum had also been removed. There was no blood. Three weeks later another cow mutilation was discovered in Dawson, this time with the familiar pattern of facial mutilation – cheek and tongue were removed, along with the vagina and rectum. The grisly finds continued throughout

February. As well as the UFOs and mutilations, police were receiving reports of unmarked helicopters flying over the scenes of mutilations. Instances of the circumstantial link between UFOs and mutilations crop up almost as often as the mutilations themselves. The Alabama wave of 1993 is just one of the better substantiated occurrences. If the mutilators are extraterrestrial, what could their purpose be?

The notion of alien creatures coming to earth to gather scientific specimens is a popular mainstay of science fiction as in the blockbuster movie, *ET*. The idea ties in well with the testimony of UFO abductees, with their frequent references to operating tables and scientific examinations. The crucial difference is, of course, that no abductees are partially dissected then dumped where they were found. If the mutilators really were aliens, why would they make this distinction?

There remain many unexplained features to the appearance of animal mutilations all over the world, not least the uniformity of their methods. Some of these "mysteries" do have at least partial scientific explanations. Animals such as cows and horses have a defence mechanism that triggers when they feel that they are under attack by predators. Capillaries in the skin and muscle shrink down and blood is pooled in the vital internal organs. In this way, a cow that has escaped a predator with only a mauling can avoid bleeding to death. This goes some way to explaining the bloodless hide-deep cuts found on many mutilated cattle. It does not, however, explain the lack of blood when these vital internal organs are also removed.

The animal mutilation phenomenon is one of the best documented mysteries in the world. Police reports exist

119

for thousands of cases worldwide. Even the most terrestrial of explanations, such as a Satanic cult or secret society, are so fantastic as to seem impossible. In these circumstances, is it really more incredible to say that our livestock is being attacked by UFOs?

Crop Circles

On August 15, 1980, the *Wiltshire Times* carried an odd report concerning the apparently wanton vandalism of a field of oats near Westbury in Wiltshire, England. The owner of the field, John Scull, had found his oats crushed to the ground in three separate areas, all within sight of the famous White Horse of Westbury – a hillside figure cut into the chalk. It seemed obvious to Scull that the crops had been damaged by people rather than natural phenomena since the areas were identical in shape and size: almost perfect circles, each 60 feet in diameter. It was also noted that the circles had apparently been produced manually rather than mechanically, since there was no sign that any kind of machinery had been moved through the field. In fact, there seemed to be no evidence of *anything* crossing the field – the circles were surrounded by undamaged oats, with no paths that would indicate intruders. One speculation was that the vandals had used stilts.

Close examination of the flattened cereal revealed that the circles had not been made at the same time – that, in fact, the damage had been spread over a period of two or three months, probably between May and the end of July. The edges of the circles were sharply defined and all the grain within the circles was flattened in the same

Corn circles seen in Espoo, Helsinki, September 21, 1996

direction, creating a clockwise swirling effect around the centers. None of the oats had been cut – merely flattened. The effect might have been produced by a very tall, strong man standing in the center of each circle and swinging a heavy weight around on a long piece of rope.

Dr Terence Meaden, an atmospheric physicist from nearby Bradford-on-Avon and a senior member of the Tornado and Storm Research Organization (TORRO), suggested that the circles had been produced by a summer whirlwind. Such wind effects are not uncommon on open farmland. But Dr Meaden had to admit that he had never seen or heard of a whirlwind creating circles. Whirlwinds tend to scud about randomly, pausing for only a few seconds in any one place, so one might expect a random pathway through the crop.

Another interesting fact was noted by Ian Mrzyglod, editor of the "anomaly" magazine *The PROBE Report*. The "center point" on all three circles was actually off-center by as much as four feet. The swirling patterns around these points were therefore oval, not circular. This seemed to contradict the vandal theory – vandals would hardly go to the trouble of creating precise ellipses. It also made Meaden's whirlwind explanation seem less plausible.

Almost a year later, on August 19, 1981, another three-circle formation appeared in a wheatfield below Cheesefoot Head, near Winchester in Hampshire. These circles had been created simultaneously and, unlike the widely dispersed circles in Wiltshire, were in close formation – one circle 60 feet across with two 25-foot circles on either side. But the sides of these circles had the same precise edges as the Wiltshire circles, and again, the swirl of the flattened plants was slightly off-center, creating ellipses.

And, again, there were no paths through the grain to indicate intruders.

The new evidence seemed to undermine the natural-causes theory. Instead of a neat, stationary whirlwind creating only one circle, Meaden now had to argue the existence of an atmospheric disturbance that hops-cotched across the landscape and produced circles of different sizes. Meaden suggested that perhaps peculiarities of terrain created this effect – the field in question was on a concave, "punchbowl" slope, and this might indeed have caused the vortex to "jump."

There were a few isolated reports of similar incidents in 1982, but they were unspectacular and excited little attention. As if to make up for it, a series of five-circle phenomena began in 1983, one of them at Bratton, again close to the White Horse of Westbury. These were clearly not caused by whirlwinds, for they consisted of one large circle with four smaller ones spaced around it like the number five on a die. A "quintuplet" appeared in Cley Hill, near Warminster – a town that, in earlier years, had had more than its share of "flying saucer" sightings. Another appeared in a field below Ridgeway near Wantage in Oxfordshire. Quintuplets were no longer freaks but were virtually the norm.

Now the national press began to cover the phenomena. The British press often refer to the summer as the "silly season" because, for some odd reason, there is often a shortage of good news stories in the hot months of the year, and newspapers tend to make up for the deficiency by blowing up trivia into major news stories. Crop circles answered the need perfectly, with the result that the British public soon became familiar with the strange circle formations. UFO enthusiasts appeared on television explaining their view that the phenomena could be explained only by flying saucers. Skeptics preferred the notion of fraud.

This latter view seemed to be confirmed when a second quintuplet found at Bratton turned out to be a hoax sponsored by the *Daily Mirror* newspaper; a family named Shepherd had been paid to duplicate the other Bratton circles. They did this by entering the field on stilts and trampling the crops underfoot. But, significantly, the hoax was quickly detected by Bob Rickard, the editor of an anomaly magazine, *Fortean Times*, who noted the telltale signs of human intruders which had not been present in earlier circles, and the fact that the edges of the circles were quite rough and imprecise. The aim of the hoax was to embarrass the competing tabloid, the *Daily Express*, which had originally scooped the crop circle story.

Over the next two years, the number of circles increased, as did their complexity. There were crop circles with "rings" around them – flattened pathways several feet wide that ran around the outer edge in a neat circle. Some were even found with two or three such rings. At the same time the quintuplet formations and "singletons" also continued to appear.

It began to look as if whoever – or whatever – was creating the circles took pleasure in taunting the investigators. When believers in the whirlwind theory pointed out that the swirling had so far been clockwise, a counterclockwise circle promptly appeared. When it was suggested that a hoaxer might be making the circles with the aid of a helicopter, a crop circle was found directly beneath a power line. When an aerial photographer named Busty Taylor was flying home after photographing crop circles and mentioned that he would like to see a formation in the shape of a Celtic cross, a Celtic cross appeared the next day in the field over which he had been flying. And, as if to rule out all possibility that natural causes could be responsible, one "sextuplet" in Hampshire in 1990 had keylike objects sticking out of the sides of three circles, producing the impression of an ancient pictogram. Another crop "pattern" of 1990 (at Chilcomb), seemed to represent a kind of chemical retort with a long neck, with four rectangles neatly spaced on either side of it, making nonsense of Meaden's insistence that the circles were caused by "natural atmospheric forces."

Rickard brought together a number of eyewitness descriptions of the actual appearance of circles:

Suddenly the grass began to sway before our eyes and laid itself flat in a clockwise spiral . . . . A perfect circle was completed in less than half a minute, all the time accompanied by a high-pitched humming sound . . . . My attention was drawn to a "wave" coming through the heads of the cereal crop in a straight line . . . . The agency, though invisible, behaved like a solid object . . . . When we reached the spot where the circles had been, we were suddenly caught up in a terrific whirlwind . . . . [The dog] went wild . . . . There was a rushing sound and a rumble . . . . then suddenly everything was still . . . . It was uncanny . . . . The dawn chorus stopped; the sky darkened . . . .

The high-pitched humming sound may be significant. It was noted on another occasion, on June 16, 1991, when a 75-foot circle (with a "bull's-eye" in the center), appeared on Bolberry Down, near Salcombe in Devon. A local ham-radio operator named Lew Dilling was tuned into a regular frequency when strange high-pitched blips and clicks emerged. He recognized the sounds as being the same as others that had been heard in connection with crop-circle incidents. "The signals were so powerful," said Dilling, "that you could hear them in the background of Radio Moscow and Voice of America – and they would normally swamp everything."

The landlord of the local pub, Sean Hassall, learned of the crop circle indirectly when his spaniel went berserk and began tearing up the carpet, doing considerable damage.

The owner of the field, Dudley Stidson, was alerted to the circle by two walkers. He went to the six-acre hayfield and found a giant circle in the center. But this one differed from many such circles in that the hay was burned, as if someone had put a huge hot-plate on it. Stidson emphasized that there was no sign of intrusion in the field, such as trampled wheat. Another local farmer, Peter Goodall, found a 60-foot circle in his winter wheat (at Matford Barton), at the same time.

A few days before these incidents occurred, a Japanese professor announced that he had solved the crop-circle mystery. Professor Yoshihiko Ohtsuki, of Tokyo's Waseda University, had created an "elastic plasma" fireball – a very strong form of ionized air – in the laboratory. When the fireball touched a plate covered with aluminium powder, it created beautiful circles and rings in the powder. Ohtsuki suggested that plasma fireballs were created by atmospheric conditions and that they would flatten crops as they descended toward the ground. This certainly sounded as if it could be the solution of the mystery – until it was recalled that some of the crop circles had rectangles or keylike objects sticking out of their sides. Another objection was that fireballs are usually about the size of footballs and are clearly visible. Surely a fireball with a 75-foot diameter would be visible for many miles? And why were no fireballs seen by the eyewitnesses cited by Rickard, who simply saw the corn being flattened in a clockwise circle?

Another recent suggestion is that an excess of fertilizer will cause the corn on which it is used to shoot up much faster than that which surrounds it, after which it will collapse and lie flat. There are two objections to this theory – Why would a farmer spray an excess of fertilizer in a circle – or some even more complicated design? And why would the corn collapse in a clockwise direction?

In a symposium entitled "The Crop Circle Enigma" (1990), John Michell made the important suggestion that the crop circles have a meaning and that "the meaning . . . . is to be found in the way people are affected by them." In conjunction with this idea, Michell noted that "Jung discerned the meaning of UFOs as agents and portents of changes in human thought patterns, and that function has been clearly inherited by crop circles."

In order to understand this fully, we have to bear in mind Jung's concept of "synchronicity" or "meaningful coincidence." His view is basically that "meaningful coincidences" are somehow *created* by the unconscious mind – probably with the intention of jarring the conscious mind into a keener state of perception. Preposterous synchronicities imbue us with a powerful sense that there *is* a hidden meaning behind everyday reality. Certain pessimistically inclined writers – such as

Shakespeare and Thomas Hardy – have taken the view that accidents and disasters indicate a kind of malevolent intelligence behind life. Jung's view is that synchronicities produce a sense of a *benevolent* intelligence behind life. He once suggested that the UFO phenomenon was an example of what he called "projection" – that is, of a physical effect somehow produced by the unconscious mind, in fact, by the "collective unconscious."

Michell was, in effect, suggesting that the crop-circle phenomenon serves the same purpose. Yet to say, as he did, that the crop circles have a "meaning" could also imply that some "other intelligence" is trying to influence human thought patterns. This is an idea that has been current since the earliest UFO sightings in the late 1940s and was popularized by Arthur C. Clarke in the screenplay of the film *2001: A Space Odyssey* – specifically, the notion that "higher intelligences" have been involved in the evolution of the human brain.

The logical objection to this theory is that to "make" man evolve is a contradiction in terms; evolution is the result of an *inner* drive. Presumably, a higher intelligence would recognize this better than we do. Yet it is also true that intelligence evolves through a sense of curiosity, of mystery, and that such apparent absurdities as flying saucers and crop circles certainly qualify as mysteries.

Michell concluded by quoting Jung's words that UFOs are "signs of great changes to come which are compatible with the end of an era." And whether or not Jung was correct, there can be no doubt that the UFO phenomenon has played an enormous part in the transformation of human consciousness from the narrow scientific materialism of the first half of the twentieth century to the much more open-minded attitude of its second half. Whether or not the crop circles prove to have a "natural" explanation, this may be their ultimate significance in the history of the late twentieth century.

6

The Theories

So what are flying saucers? Many theories have been put forward to explain them. Most common is the idea that they are the spacecraft of some extraterrestrial intelligent life-form. The main problem with this answer is that it begs more questions. Where do these creatures come from? How long have they been visiting us? Are they life as we understand it, or something totally beyond our experience?

Chariots of the Gods?

Published in 1965, Erich von Daniken's book *Chariots of the Gods?* caused a flurry of interest and immediately became an international bestseller. Daniken had recognized that the best way to present controversial ideas is to state them dogmatically in words of one syllable. His book begins, "It took courage to write this book, and it will take courage to read it." Neither statement is true, but it gives the reader a sense of instant involvement. Daniken quickly goes on to state his main thesis. "Nevertheless, one thing is certain . . . . the past teemed with unknown Gods who visited the primeval earth in manned spaceships. Incredible technical achievements existed in the past. There is a mass of know-how which we have only partially rediscovered today."

Daniken weaves his theories out of the familiar materials, The Great Pyramid, the Nazca lines in Peru, the ancient legends of giants and gods, the Piri Reis map. An American professor, Charles Hapgood, had become so intrigued by the Piri Reis map, and other maps dating from the middle ages, that he had given them to his students as a study project. They had reached some remarkable conclusions – for example, that the South Pole, as shown in the Piri Reis map, had been drawn *before the Pole was covered with ice*, which must have been at least 6,000 years ago, and possibly as many as 9,000. Daniken makes full use of such strange anomalies. But he also adds a great deal of speculation, a mass of unassimilated facts, and some downright inventions. He takes from George Hunt Williamson the idea that the pyramids were built by spacemen – on the grounds that they are too massive to have been built by human beings, but he somehow manages to multiply their weight by five. He explains that the engineering problems would have been beyond men who knew nothing about the use of rope – although there are rope-making scenes on the walls of Egyptian tombs dating long before the building of the Great Pyramid. He suggests that the Nazca lines are giant runways, without pausing to reflect that even the most powerful modern aircraft does not need a runway several miles long. (In any case, the lines drawn on the desert are only scratched on its surface, and would quickly be blown in all directions if a plane attempted to land on them.)

At times, his information seems to be wilfully distorted. Chapter 5 of *Chariots of the Gods?* begins with an account of the Assyrian *Epic of Gilgamesh*, "a sensational find that was made in the hill of Kuyundjik around the turn of the century." (In fact, the *Epic* was discovered by Hormuzd Rassam, an assistant of the great archaeologist Layard, in 1853, and further missing portions were unearthed 20 years later.) The aim of Daniken's retelling is to demonstrate that the ancient races of Mesopotamia knew about spaceships, so he describes how the sun god seized the hero Enkidu in his claws and bore him upward with such velocity that his body felt as heavy as lead – which, as Daniken rightly observes, seems to show an astonishing knowledge of the effect of acceleration. A visit to the tower of the goddess Ishtar (Innanis) is described, implying that it is a space vehicle, and then "the first eye witness account of a spaceship" in which Enkidu flies for four hours in the brazen talons of an eagle and describes the earth as seen from the air.

Anyone who takes the trouble to check the Gilgamesh *Epic* will discover that all these episodes appear to have been imagined by Daniken – nothing remotely resembling them is to be found in it. The sun god (Shamash) does not seize Enkidu in his talons, there is no visit to the tower of the goddess Ishtar (she only makes one appearance in the *Epic* as the attempted seductress of Gilgamesh), there is no four-hour space trip in the claws of an eagle.

Daniken also tells us that "the door spoke like a living person", and that we can unhesitatingly identify this with a loudspeaker! He goes on to say that Gilgamesh asks whether Enkidu has been smitten by the poisonous breath of a heavenly beast (i.e. has breathed in the fumes of a spaceship), and asks how Gilgamesh could possibly know that a "heavenly beast" could cause fatal and incurable disease. The answer is that he couldn't, for he does not ask the question. Neither does the loudspeaker doorway make any kind of appearance in Gilgamesh!

Daniken's books provide, to put it kindly, plenty of examples of intellectual carelessness combined with wishful thinking and a casual attitude towards logic. In *Gold of the Gods*, he offers a photograph of a skeleton carved out of stone and wants to know, "Were there anatomists who dissected bodies for the prehistoric sculptor? As we know, Wilhelm Conrad Rontgen did not discover the new kind of rays he called X-rays until 1895!" It never seems to have occurred to him that every graveyard must have been full of skeletons.

Perhaps the most obvious example of his carelessness was his treatment of Easter Island. Daniken alleged that the island's gigantic statues – some of them 20 feet high – could only have been carved and erected with the aid of sophisticated technology, which would have been far beyond the resources of primitive savages. In fact, the Norwegian explorer, Thor Heyerdahl, persuaded modern Easter Islanders to carve and erect statues with their own "primitive technology." Von Daniken had also pointed out that Easter Island has no wood for rollers – unaware that only a few centuries ago, the island was covered with woodland and that the Easter Islanders have been responsible for the destruction of their own environment.

The von Daniken bubble finally burst in 1972, when, in *Gold of the Gods*, the author claimed to have visited a vast underground cave system in Ecuador, with elaborately engineered walls, and examined an ancient library engraved on metal sheets. When his fellow explorer,

Juan Moricz, denied that von Daniken had ever entered the caves, von Daniken admitted that his account was fictional, but argued that his book was not intended to be a scientific treatise. Since it was designed for popular consumption, he had allowed himself a certain degree of poetic license. Yet in a biography of Daniken, Peter Krassa ignores this admission, insisting that the case is still open and that Daniken may have been telling the truth after all.

In fact, a British expedition to the caves found them to be natural, with evidence of habitation by primitive man but with no signs of Daniken's ancient library or perfectly engineered walls. A two-hour TV exposé of von Daniken subsequently punctured every one of his major claims.

The Dogon

Yet in spite of Daniken's absurdities, it has to be admitted that there is a certain amount of evidence for the "ancient astronaut" theory. Members of an African tribe called the Dogon, who live in the Republic of Mali (some 300 miles south of Timbuktu), insist that they possess knowledge that was transmitted to them by "spacemen" from the star Sirius, which is 8.7 lightyears away. Dogon mythology insists that the "Dog Star" Sirius (so called because it is in the constellation Canis), has a dark companion that is invisible to the naked eye, and that it is dense and very heavy. This is correct; Sirius does indeed have a dark companion known as Sirius B.

The existence of Sirius B had been suspected by astronomers since the mid-nineteenth century, and it was first observed in 1862 – although it was not described in detail until the 1920s. Is it possible that some white traveller took the knowledge of Sirius B to Africa sometime since the 1850s? It is possible but unlikely. Two French anthropologists, Marcelle Griaule and Germaine Dieterlen, first revealed the "secret of the Dogon" in an obscure paper in 1950. It was entitled "a Sudanese Sirius System" and was published in the *Journal de la Societé des Africainistes*.

The two anthropologists had lived among the Dogon since 1931, and in 1946, Griaule was initiated into the religious secrets of the tribe. He was told that fish-like creatures called the Nomo had come to earth from Sirius to civilize its people. Sirius B, which the Dogon call *Po Tolo* (naming it after the seed that forms the staple part of their diet, and whose botanical name is *Digitaria*), is made of matter heavier than any on earth and moves in an eliptical orbit, taking 50 years to do so. It was not until 1928 that Sir Arthur Eddington postulated the theory of "white dwarfs" – stars whose atoms have collapsed inward, so that a piece the size of a pea could weigh half a ton. (Sirius B is the size of the earth yet weighs as much as the sun.) Griaule and Dieterlen went to live among the Dogon three years later. Is it likely that some traveller carried a new and complex scientific theory to a remote African tribe in the three years between 1928 and 1931?

An oriental scholar named Robert Temple went to Paris to study the Dogon with Germaine Dieterlen. He soon concluded that the knowledge shown by the Dogon could not be explained away as coincidence or "defusion" (knowledge passed on through contact with other peoples.) The Dogon appeared to have an extraordinarily detailed knowledge of our solar system. They said that the moon was "dry and dead," and they drew Saturn with a ring around it (which, of course, is only visible through a telescope.) They knew that the planets revolved around the sun. They knew about the moons of Jupiter (first seen through a telescope by Galileo.) They had recorded the movements of Venus in their temples. They knew that the earth rotates and that the number of stars is infinite. And when they drew the eliptical orbit of Sirius, they showed the star off-center, not in the middle of the orbit – as someone without knowledge of astronomy would naturally conclude.

The Dogon insist that their knowledge was brought to them by the amphibious Nomo from a "star" (presumably they meant a planet) which, like Sirius B, rotates around Sirius and whose weight is only a quarter of Sirius B's. They worshipped the Nomo as gods. They drew diagrams to portray the spinning of the craft in which these creatures landed and were precise about the landing location as the place to the northwest of present Dogon country, where the Dogon originated. They mentioned that the "ark" in which the Nomo arrived caused a whirling dust storm and that it "skidded." They speak of "a flame that went out as they touched the earth," which implies that they landed in a small space capsule. Dogon mythology also mentions a glowing object in the sky like a star, presumably the mother ship. Our telescopes have not yet revealed the "planet" of the Nomo, but that is hardly surprising. Sirius B was only discovered because its weight caused perturbations in the orbit of Sirius. The Dog Star is 35.5 times as bright (and hot) as our sun, so any planet capable of supporting life would have to be in the far reaches of its solar system and would almost certainly be invisible to telescopes. Temple surmises that the planet of the Nomo would be hot and steamy and that this probably explains why intelligent life evolved in its seas, which would be cooler. These fish-people would spend much of their time on land but close to the water. They would need a layer of water on their skins to be comfortable, and if their skins dried, it would be as agonising as severe sunburn. Temple sees them as a kind of dolphin.

But what were such creatures doing in the middle of the desert near Timbuktu? In fact, the idea is obviously absurd. Temple points out that to the northwest of Mali lies Egypt, and for many reasons, he is inclined to believe that the landing of the Nomo took place there. Temple also points out that a Babylonian historian named Berossus – a contemporary and apparently an acquaintance of Aristotle (fourth century BC) – claims in his history, of which only fragments survive, that Babylonian civilisation was founded by alien amphibians, the chief of whom is Oannes – the Philistines knew him as Dagon (and the science fiction writer H. P. Lovecraft borrowed him for his own mythology.) The Greek grammarian, Apollodorus (about 140 BC), had apparently read more of Berossus, for he criticizes another Greek writer, Abydenus, for failing to mention that Oannes was only one of the "fish-people". He calls these aliens "annedoti" ("repulsive ones") and says they are "semi-demons" from the sea.

Why should the Dogon pay any particular attention to Sirius, even though it was one of the brightest stars in the sky? After all, it was merely one of thousands of stars. There, at least, the skeptics can produce a convincing answer. Presumably, the Dogon learned from the Egyptians, and for the ancient Egyptians, Sothis (as they called Sirius) was the most important star in the heavens – at least after 3200 BC, when it began to rise just before the dawn, at the beginning of the Egyptian new year and signalled that the Nile was about to rise.

So the "Dog Star" became the god of the rising waters. The goddess Sothis was identified with Isis; and Temple points out that in Egyptian tomb paintings, Isis is usually to be found in a boat with two fellow goddesses, Anukis and Satis. Temple argues convincingly that this indicates that the Egyptians knew Sirius to be a three-star system – the unknown "Sirius sea" being the home of the Nomo. An ancient Arabic name for one of the stars in the Sirian constellation (not Sirius itself), is Al Wazn, meaning "wait," and one text said that it is almost too heavy to rise above the horizon.

Temple suggests that the ancients may have looked towards the Canis constellation for Sirius B and mistaken it for Al Wazn. He also suggests that Homer's Sirens – mermaidlike creatures who are all-knowing and who try to lure men away from their everyday responsibilities – are actually "Sirians," amphibious goddesses. He also points out that Jason's boat, the Argo, is associated with the goddess Isis and that it has 50 rowers – 50 being the number of years it takes Sirius B to circle Sirius A. There are many other fish-bodied aliens in Greek mythology, including the Telchines of Rhodes, who were supposed to have come from the sea and to have introduced men to various arts, including metalwork. Significantly, they had dogs' heads.

But if the Egyptians knew about Sirius B and the Nomo, then why do we not have Egyptian texts that tell us about aliens from the "Dog Star" system? Here the answer is obvious. Marcelle Grialle had to be "initiated" by Dogon priests before he was permitted to learn about the visitors from Sirius. If the Egyptians knew about Sirius B, the knowledge was revealed only to initiates. But it would have left its mark in Egyptian mythology – for example, in the boat of Isis.

Temple's book *The Sirius Mystery* (1976), is full of such "mythological evidence," and much of it has been attacked for stretching interpretation too far. Yet what remains when all the arguments have been considered is the curious fact that a remote African tribe has some precise knowledge of an entire star system not visible to the human eye alone and that they attribute this knowledge to aliens from that star system. That single fact suggests that in spite of Daniken's absurdities, we should remain open-minded about the possibility of alien visitors who once landed on our planet.

Jung on Flying Saucers

In 1958, the psychologist Carl Jung entered the controversy with a book called *Flying Saucers: a Modern Myth of Things Seen in the Skies*. Jung's theory is that flying saucers are what he calls "projections" – which is another name for illusions or hallucinations. He believes that these "projections" originate in what he calls the "collective unconscious" – that is, a deep stratum of the unconscious mind that is full of the basic myths and symbols of the human race. Jung sees great significance in the fact that flying saucers are circular – like mandalas – the Tibetan religious symbol of a "mystic circle," which is also found in most religions of the world.

Carl Jung

According to Jung, man has a religious craving – what he calls "the religious function" – which is as deep as the sexual needs emphasized by Freud. This craving is basically a need for personal evolution, or what Jung calls "individuation." So, according to Jung, the flying saucer is basically a projection of modern man's craving for a savior – for some kind of religious evolution.

But there is a complication. Jung admits that UFOs can be photographed and cause images on radar screens. Then how *can* they be "projections" – if a projection is basically an illusion? Jung leaves that question unanswered, but he implies that under certain conditions, a "projection" *can* cause physical effects. In other words, the mind can affect physical reality. But Jung is careful not to underline this aspect and few of the commentaries on his book even mention it.

But one further complication is provided by an interview between Jung and the aviator, Charles Lindbergh, in the summer of 1959. "To my astonishment," said Lindbergh (in a letter to his publisher's wife), "I found that Jung accepted flying saucers as factual. On the one hand, he didn't seem in the least interested in psychological aspects. On the other, he didn't seem at all interested in factual information relating to the investigation of flying saucers reports." When Lindbergh told Jung that the US Air Force had found no evidence whatever for flying saucers, "it was obvious that he did not wish to pursue the subject further." Lindbergh persisted, pouring cold water on the sightings, and quoting his friend General Spaatz (of the US Air Force) as saying, "Don't you suppose that if there was anything true about this flying saucer business, you and I would have heard about it by this time?" Jung's reply was, "There are a great many things

141

going on around this earth that you and General Spaatz don't know about." It seems clear then, that, as in so many other cases, Jung was telling slightly less than he knew when presenting his views to the public. Significantly, Lindbergh commented, "One intuitively feels the elements of mysticism and greatness about him – even though they may have been mixed at times, with elements of charlatanism."

Are They Fairies?

In 1970, Ufologist Jacques Vallee produced one of the most startling theories about UFOs so far. In a book called *Passport to Magonia*, Vallee pointed out the many similarities between "close encounters" with flying saucers and those with fairies.

Before we go any further, it is important to recognize that the evidence for fairies – or "the little people" – is in many ways as convincing as the evidence for flying saucers. The poet W. B. Yeats, born in Ireland, spent a great deal of time in the west of Ireland investigating stories about fairies, and soon recognized that the majority of Irish country folk accepted their existence as a concrete fact of life. Yeats himself ultimately came to believe in the real existence of the "little folk." He encouraged the orientalist W. Y. Evans Wentz – best known for his translation of *The Tibetan Book of the Dead* – to study the folklore of the fairies; the result was Wentz's first book, *The Fairy Faith in Celtic Countries* (1911), one of the best books on the subject. Yeats's friend, the poet AE (George Russell), contributed an anonymous piece to the book (under the title "An Irish

Mystic's Testimony"), in which he described his own fairy sightings with a factual accuracy and precision of an anthropologist describing primitive tribes – shining beings, opalescent beings, water beings, wood beings, lower elementals. "The first of (the fairies) I saw I remember very clearly . . . . There was first a dazzle of light, and then I saw that this came from the heart of a tall figure with a body apparently shaped out of half-transparent or opalescent air, and throughout the body ran a radiant electrical fire, to which the heart seemed the center. Around the head of this being and through its waving luminous hair, which was blown all about the body like living strands of gold, there appeared flaming wing-like auras. From the being itself light seemed to stream outwards in every direction; and the effect left on me after the vision was one of extraordinary lightness, joyousness or ecstasy."

At the end of his book, Wentz concludes that the factual and scientific evidence for the real existence of fairies is overwhelming, that in fact "there are hundreds of proven cases of phenomena."

Many of the cases quoted by Wentz sound like cases of "second sight," the ability to see "spirits." But there have been many fairy sightings that make them seem much more down to earth. A psychic called Lois Bourne, in her book *Witch Among Us*, describes her own sighting of one of the "little people" in Cornwall. During an evening with a member of a "wicca" coven, she and her husband Wilfred were asked if they would like to see a goblin. The host explained that one appeared among the rushes of the mill stream at Treago Mill, Cuberts Heath, every morning at sunrise. If they wanted to see him, they would have to be up early. The next morning Lois and her husband joined their host at the mill gate and crept up the stream. She writes, "I have never been able to decide, and still cannot decide, whether I really saw that goblin, or if Rob made me see it . . . . Whatever it was there, sitting on a stone calmly washing his socks, was an elfin creature with a red hat, green coat and trews, one yellow sock on and the other one in his tiny hands, in the process of being washed. I remember thinking at the time, in my sleepy, befuddled, but practical way 'what an atrocious color combination.' Suddenly he saw us and he disappeared . . . . 'Now do you believe me?' asked Rob."

Vallee tells how, at 11.00 a.m. of April 18, 1961, a 60-year-old chicken farmer named Joe Simonton, who lived near Eagle River, Wisconsin, was attracted out of his house by a peculiar noise similar to "nobby tyres on a wet pavement." In his yard there was a silvery saucer-shaped object, "brighter than chrome," which appeared to be hovering close to the ground without touching it. It was about 12 feet high and 30 feet in diameter. A hatch opened about five feet from the ground, and Simonton saw three men inside the machine. They were about five feet tall, and dressed in black. Simonton said they appeared to look like Italians.

One of them held up a jug made of chrome and signalled to Joe Simonton that he needed water. Simonton filled it inside the house and when he returned, saw that one of the men inside the saucer was "frying food on a flameless grill of some sort." The interior of the ship was black. Simonton could see several instrument panels and heard a slow whining noise like the hum of a generator. When he made a motion indicating that he was interested in the food, one of the men who was also dressed in black handed him three cookies, about three inches in diameter and perforated with small holes. After a few minutes, the door closed in such a way that its outline was almost undetectable and the object arose 20 feet from the ground before taking off, causing a blast of air that bowed nearby trees.

Simonton went along to the offices of the Food and Drug Laboratory of the US Department of Health, Education and Welfare, and asked them to analyze one of the cookies. The laboratory concluded that the material was an ordinary pancake of terrestrial origin. Two deputies sent by the sheriff, who had known Simonton for 14 years, arrived at the scene but could not find any evidence of the saucer. But the sheriff commented that it was obvious that Simonton believed in the truth of what he was saying and talked very sensibly.

Vallee then goes on to talk about Wentz's book on the fairy faith, and quotes the story of Pat Feeney, who described how one day, a little woman came to his house and asked for oatmeal. "Paddy had so little that he was ashamed to offer it, so he offered her some potatoes instead, but she wanted oatmeal, and then he gave her all that he had. She told him to place it back in the bin till she should return for it. This he did and the next morning the bin was overflowing with oatmeal. The woman was one of the Gentry."

Like Yeats, Wentz was able to pick up dozens of factual accounts of the Gentry, "When I was a young man I often used to go out in the mountains over there to fish for trout or hunt. And it was in January on a cold, dry day while carrying my gun that I and a friend with me as we were walking around Ben Bulben saw one of the Gentry for the first time . . . . This one was dressed in blue with a head-dress adorned with what seemed to be frills. When he came upon us, he said to me in a sweet and silvery voice, 'The seldom you come to this mountain the better, Mister, a young lady here wants to take you away.'

"Then he told us not to fire our guns, because the Gentry disliked being disturbed by the noise. And he seemed to be like a soldier of the Gentry on guard. As we were leaving the mountain, he told us not to look back and we didn't."

Vallee also tells the strange story of the Madonna of Guadalupe. In 1531, a 57-year-old Aztec Indian called Singing Eagle (whose Spanish name was Juan Diego), was going to church in Tlaltelolco, near Mexico City. Suddenly the air was full of sweet bird song, and since it was a freezing December morning, he was puzzled. Then someone with a harmonious voice called his name from the top of a hill. When he climbed the hill, he saw "a young Mexican girl about 14-years-old and wonderfully beautiful." There were golden beams around her, although the sun was still below the horizon. She told Juan Diego that her name was Mary and she wanted a temple at that particular place, "so run now to Tenochtitlan (later Mexico City) and tell the Lord Bishop all that you have seen and heard."

In great embarrassment, the poor Indian went to the Bishop's palace. He succeeded in gaining an audience with the Bishop, but, just as he expected, the Bishop obviously thought he was mad. On his way home, he once again met the lady and told her that he should send a more suitable messenger. She replied that she had chosen him and that he had to go back to the Bishop again the next day. "Tell him it is the Virgin Mary who sends you."

Juan Diego went back to the Bishop's Palace the next day and the Bishop, whose name was Fray Juan de Zumarraga, was impressed by his air of honesty. He told Juan to ask the apparition for some sign and then told two servants to follow him secretly. They followed him up the hill, at which point he vanished. (Vallee points out that this sounds exactly like a traditional fairy tale, with a human being vanishing into a fairy hill.)

In fact, Juan saw the lady again and told him to come back the following day at daybreak, when he would be given a sign for the Bishop. However, the next morning, Juan's uncle – his only relative – was seriously ill, and Juan spent the day trying to relieve his sufferings. As he set out to find a priest the following morning, he met the lady again and when he explained why he had failed to keep the appointment, was relieved when she said, "Are you not under my shadow and protection? Your uncle will not die this time. At this very moment his health is restored. There is now no reason for your journey and you can peacefully attend to mine. Go to the top of the hill, cut the flowers you will find there, and bring them to me." And at the top of the hill, on a midwinter day, Juan found Castilian roses, "their petals wet with dew." He placed these in his Indian cape (*tilma*). The lady arranged the flowers in his cape, then tied it behind his neck so the roses would not fall out.

At the Bishop's palace, the servants made fun of Juan but when they tried to grab some of the roses, they were baffled as the flowers seemed to dissolve in their fingers. Eventually, Juan was allowed to see the Bishop. As he untied his tilma, the flowers fell in an untidy heap on the floor, but this was evidently not the sign that the lady had intended. The tilma now had a beautiful picture of the Virgin embroidered on it in bright colors. The bishop fell on his knees before it, and then followed Juan Diego to the hill where he had seen the Virgin. The church was accordingly built there – the hill is called Tepeyac – in her name, and above the altar, Juan Diego's tilma is still (after more than four centuries), as bright and unfaded as ever.

The natural tendency of the skeptic is to dismiss this as a story invented to explain a particularly beautiful piece of woven cloth. But Vallee is more concerned in pointing out the similarity of this "myth" and so many sightings of "little people" and UFOs. He also points out that many other religious "apparitions" bear a strong resemblance to UFOs hovering in the sky.

Vallee adds another interesting speculation to his story of the Guadalupe Madonna. Why Guadalupe, which is a small town in a mountain range in Spain? Vallee suggests that the Indian word used by the apparition was *tetlcoatlaxopeuh*, which would be transcribed phonetically as *deguatlashhupee*, which to a Spaniard would sound like "de Guadalupe." But the original word *tetlcoatlaxopeuh* means "stone serpent trodden on." The stone serpent – quetzalcoatl – is the image of the ancient Mayan god, so "stone serpent trodden on" may mean that *quetzalcoatl* has been supplanted by the Christian religious symbol. The story unites the religion of ancient Mexico with modern Christianity. Vallee also points out that the sweet sound of birds heard by Juan Diego is like the "sweet music" described so often in accounts of those who claim to have encountered the faery.

In a later book, *The Invisible College* (1975), later reissued under the title of *UFOs: The Psychic Solution* (1977), Vallee expands his thesis about religious "apparitions" to include those of Lourdes, Fatima and Knock. What Vallee appears to be saying is that UFO activity should not be taken as a simple material phenomenon, like meteorites. Like Jung, he feels that it is closely connected with the mentality of those who observe it. And just as a religious apparition can be interpreted into ways: (1) wishful thinking by religiously-inclined people and (2) a genuine intervention from the "world of the spirit," so he feels that UFOs can be regarded as delusions or as some kind of "intervention" whose purpose is connected with causing a change in human consciousness. He calls the last chapter of his book "The Control System," and compares UFO sightings to the thermostats that regulate the temperature in our houses. "I propose the hypothesis that there is a control system for human consciousness. I have not determined whether it is natural or spontaneous; whether it is explainable in terms of genetics, of social psychology, or of ordinary phenomena – or if it is artificial in nature, and under the power of some superhuman will. It may be entirely determined by laws that we have not yet discovered."

Here, then, we have moved a long way from the simplistic view that UFOs are either a manifestation of dangerous aliens who wish to colonize our earth, or that they are benevolent aliens who wish to educate the human race. Like Jung, Vallee appears to be suggesting that there is some form of "other reality" – and that their purpose is to make human beings aware of some other level of reality.

John Keel on UFOs

John Keel is a New York journalist whose original attitude towards flying saucers was skeptical. But in 1953, in Egypt, he saw his first UFO, a metallic disc with a revolving rim hovering over the Aswan dam in daylight. Yet even so, it was not until 1966 that he decided to undertake a careful study of the subject, and subscribed to a press-cutting agency. What then staggered him was the sheer number of the sightings – he often received 150 in a day. Moreover, it soon became clear that even these were only a small percentage of the total, and that thousands of sightings were going unrecorded. What also fascinated Keel was that so many witnesses who had seen UFOs from their cars had later seen them over their homes – this suggested that the "spacemen" were not merely alien scientists or explorers, engaged in routine surveying work, but that they took an active interest in the people with whom they made "contact."

In 1967, Keel was driving along the Long Island expressway when he saw a sphere of light in the sky, presumably of course, parallel to his own. When he reached Huntington, he found that cars were parked along the roads and dozens of people were staring at four lights that were bobbing and weaving in the sky – the light that had followed Keel joined the other four. Keel was in fact on his way to interview a scientist, Phillip Burchhardt, who had seen a UFO hovering above some trees close to his home on the previous evening, and had examined it through binoculars. He had seen that it was a silvery disc illuminated by rectangular lights that blinked on and off.

Keel was impressed by the witnesses he interviewed – most were ordinary people who had no obvious reason for inventing a story about UFOs. His study of the actual literature convinced him that it was 98 per cent nonsense. But most individual witnesses were obviously telling the truth. Keel had soon accumulated enough cases to fill a 2,000-page typescript which had to be severely edited before it was published under the title *UFOs: Operation Trojan Horse.* As the title suggests, Keel was inclined to see the phenomenon as the beginning of some alien invasion. He concludes in a later book that "our little planet seems to be experiencing the interpenetration of forces or entities from some other space-time continuum."

The essence of Keel's views can be found in his book *The Mothman Prophesies.* This describes his investigations into various UFO sightings in West Virginia in 1966–67. He reports numerous sightings of a huge figure – about seven feet tall – with red eyes and gigantic wings folded on its back. It was able to keep up with fast cars without even flapping its wings. It was seen by two young couples near an old ammunition dump on November, 15, 1966, and again by a girl called Connie Carpenter, 12 days later. Connie Carpenter's eyes became red and swollen, as if from some kind of radiation, after she had seen the creature's red eyes at close quarters. In the spring of the following year, a young couple making love naked in the back of a car, saw a large ball of bluish fire hovering near the car. The next morning, both were heavily "sunburned" and had red swollen eyes. Keel's book is full of similar electronic oddities. Calls come through on disconnected telephones, police messages are picked up on switched-off radios, films and tape recordings turn out to be blank, cameras refuse to work when pointed at UFOs. Cows and sheep are found with their throats neatly slit and their bodies drained of blood. Pet dogs and cats disappear in large numbers. Keel found that his movements were actually anticipated by the opposition – for example, when he casually chose a motel to stay at, he found a sheaf of incomprehensible messages waiting for him at the desk.

According to himself, Keel was finally subjected to a kind of non-stop persecution by the "spacemen," with mysterious phonecalls, people impersonating him or claiming to be his secretary, and strange warning messages. He was convinced that the "spacemen" were genuine because they were able to make accurate predictions of the future. When he hypnotized a contactee in 1967, a spaceman named "Apol" began to speak through her, and made exact predictions about a number of plane crashes. "Apol" also predicted that the Pope would be knifed to death in the Middle East, and that this would be preceded by a great earthquake. He mentioned that Robert Kennedy was in great danger – Kennedy was, of course, assassinated in the following year. The plane crashes, says Keel, occurred exactly as predicted. In July 1967, the Vatican announced that the Pope would be visiting Turkey, and an earthquake killed 1,000 people there. But the Pope was not knifed to death at Istanbul Airport. It was three years later, when he landed at Manilla Airport, that a madman tried to kill him with a long knife. Fortunately the man was overpowered by guards. Keel believes that the entity simply misread the future or got the date wrong. Similarly, he was told that Martin Luther King would be shot in the throat while standing on his balcony in Memphis. The

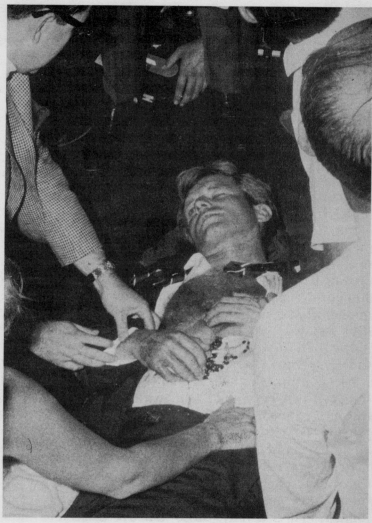

Robert Kennedy lies wounded. "Apol" had predicted he was in danger

date given was February 4, 1968. That day passed without incident – the assassination took place, exactly as described, two months later.

In long telephone conversations with Keel, "Apol" made another prophesy – there would be a massive power failure that would affect a large part of the United States on December 15. It would happen when President Johnson turned on the lights of the Christmas tree on the White House lawn. Keel watched the event on television but there was no power failure. But immediately after the President had thrown the switch, the program was interrupted for an announcement – a bridge on the Ohio river had collapsed, with great loss of life. Keel knew that the only bridge along the stretch mentioned was the Silver Bridge at Point Pleasant, the town near which all the strange occurrences had been taking place. The "spaceman" had even warned him that a major disaster would strike along the Ohio river, but implied that it would be a factory that would blow up. Keel believes that they told him the blackout story, rather than the truth, so he would have no opportunity to warn people.

Keel continues to believe that the phenomena he has observed can be violent and extremely dangerous. In this he is echoed by the British expert on UFOs, Brinsley Le Poer Trench (the Earl of Clancarty), who reached a similar conclusion in his book *Operation Earth*: ". . . . there exist at least two diametrically opposed forces of entities interested in us. Firstly, those that are the real Sky People who have been around since time immemorial. Secondly, those that live in an area indigenous to this planet, though some of us believe they also live in the interior of the earth. There is obviously a 'War in the Heavens' between these two factions. However it is not considered that battles are going on in the sense that humans usually envisage them. It is more of a mental affray for the domination of the minds of mankind."

Puharich and Geller

The late Andriya Puharich, who died in 1995, followed this same bewildering and confusing path from the normal to the paranormal.

It was as a psychologist that Puharich studied a young Dutch sculptor named Harry Stone who, when examining an ancient Egyptian pendant, fell into a trance and began drawing hieroglyphics on a sheet of paper. He also began to speak about his upbringing in ancient Egypt. An expert verified that the hieroglyphics were genuine and belonged to the period of the Pharaoh Snefru. In his book *The Sacred Mushroom*, Puharich describes the sessions in which he placed Stone under hypnosis, and of how Stone described a cult of the "Sacred Mushroom" which has now been forgotten. Next, Puharich began a series of experiments in telepathy with well-known psychics like Peter Hurkos and Eileen Garrett. *Beyond Telepathy* (1962) quickly became a classic in its field.

It was at this point that Puharich came close to destroying his career with an astonishing book called *Uri: A Journal of the Mystery of Uri Geller* (1974). This is a straightforward narrative of Puharich's three-year investigation of Geller; yet it ends by producing total confusion and bewilderment. The book begins in 1952, long before the two men met. It tells how, when Puharich was studying a Hindu psychic named Dr Vinod, the latter

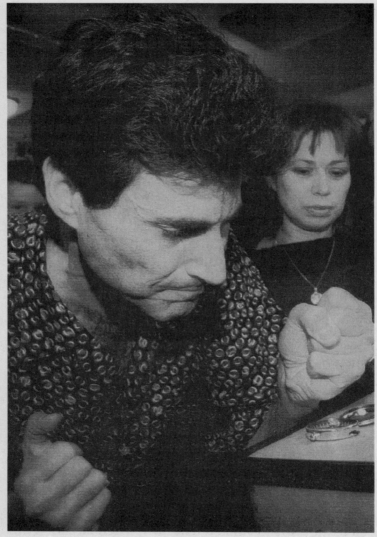

Uri Geller

began to speak in a strange voice with a perfect English accent. The voice explained that it was a member of the "Nine Principles and Forces," superhuman intelligences whose purpose is to aid human evolution.

Three years later, travelling in Mexico, Puharich met an American doctor and his wife, who also passed on lengthy messages from "space intelligences". The remarkable thing was that these messages were a continuation of the communications that had come through Dr Vinod. It began to look as if "the Nine" might really exist.

In 1963, Puharich made the acquaintance of the Brazilian "psychic surgeon" Arigo, who performed his operations with a kitchen knife which he wiped on his shirt after dealing with each case. Arigo believed he was possessed by the spirit of a dead German surgeon. According to his biographer, he had an unbroken record of successes over many years. Puharich was informed of Arigo's death in a car crash, in January 1971: he afterwards became convinced that he must have received the telephone message a quarter of an hour *before* Arigo died.

All this was a prelude to Puharich's meeting with the famous "metal bender" Uri Geller, which occurred in a Jaffa discotheque in August 1971 – two years before Geller achieved sudden fame through an appearance on BBC television. Geller's feats of telepathy and precognition impressed Puharich, and if the book was restricted to describing these feats, it would undoubtedly impress most open-minded readers. But at this point, the "extraterrestrials" reenter the story, and it turns into a chronicle of marvels and improbabilites. Placed in a trance, Geller described how, at the age of three, he had fallen asleep in a garden opposite his home and awakened to see a huge, shining figure standing over him and a bright, bowl-shaped object floating in the sky overhead. And while Geller was still hynotised, a mechanical voice began to speak from the air above his head explaining that "they" (the "space intelligences") had found Geller in the garden, and had been "programming" him ever since. Puharich, the voice said, had been selected to take care of Uri. The world was in danger of plunging into war because Egypt was planning to attack Israel, and somehow Geller and Puharich had been given the task of averting the conflict.

When Geller recovered from the trance, he grabbed the cassette on which Puharich had been recording the proceedings and Puharich swears he saw it vanish in Geller's hand. It was never recovered. This was to be a recurring pattern whenever "the Nine" communicated – they would either cause the tape to vanish or wipe the recordings from it.

It would serve no purpose to detail the marvels that fill the rest of the book. Objects are always disappearing and then reappearing. UFOs are sighted. The car engine stops and starts again for no reason. Puharich's camera bag is miraculously "teleported" 3,000 miles from New York to Tel Aviv. The war between Egypt and Israel is somehow averted, although without Puharich's intervention. This relentless succession of miracles leaves the reader bewildered and exhausted, until curiosity finally turns to a kind of punch-drunk indifference.

Understandably, the book did Geller no good at all with the general public. Instead of making converts, it turned believers into skeptics. There was something slightly comic in the assertion that Geller was the ambassador of superhuman intelligences, and that the proof lay in his ability to bend spoons. It seemed that Puharich was simply pitching Geller's claim too high, and his obvious sincerity did nothing to improve the situation. The opposition could be divided into two factions – those who believed that Geller and Puharich were trying to hoodwink the rest of the world, and those who thought Geller had hoodwinked Puharich. Not long after the book's publication, Geller and Puharich decided to go their separate ways.

At this point, one might be forgiven for assuming that the more extreme phenomena would cease. In fact – as Stuart Holroyd has revealed in a book called *Prelude to the Landing on Planet Earth* – "the Nine" apparently continued to manifest themselves as bewilderingly as ever. His story begins in 1974, when Puharich went to Florida to investigate a half-Indian psychic healer, Bobby Horne (this is not his real name.) In a hypnotic trance, Horne began to speak in a strange voice and introduced himself as an extraterrestrial intelligence named "Ancore". His purpose, he said, was to inform the human race that the space intelligences would be arriving on earth *en masse* during the next year or so and to try to prepare mankind for that traumatic event. Since the voices that had spoken through Geller had made the same claim, Puharich was understandably impressed.

Further tests took place at Ossining, New York. Others present were the author Lyall Watson, an Englishman named Sir John Whitmore, and Phyllis Schlemmer, a "psychic" who had introduced Puharich to Bobby Horne. They were told, through "Ancore," that Bobby Horne had been specially prepared for his healing tasks by having invisible wires inserted into his neck by the space intelligences. Equally startling information came through an "extraterrestrial" called "Tom," who spoke through Phyllis Schlemmer and who offered a potted history of the human race. The first civilisation was founded 32,000 years ago, in the Tarim Basin of China, by beings from space. At this time, according to "Tom," there were "three cultures, three divisions, from three areas of the universe." A more advanced civilisation was begun, then destroyed through a massacre.

This was to be the pattern of the communications for some time to come. "Ancore" spoke (through Bobby Horne) about the projected landing of UFOs, and how the space intelligences were trying to devise methods of interfering with television transmissions, so as to be able to speak directly to mankind. And Tom, speaking through Phyllis Schlemmer, went into considerable detail about earlier civilisations and the purpose of man on earth. The earth, says "Tom," is unique in the universe – every soul must pass through it sooner or later. "It is the love of this planet that generates the energy that becomes God." The earth is a kind of school, designed to teach the balance between the spiritual and the physical. But mankind has become too negative and has created a force of active evil. It has become a kind of bottleneck in the universe, blocking its evolution. Unless man evolves a new type of consciousness, or unless he receives help from outside, the earth will enter a new ice age within two centuries, due to pollution of the atmosphere.

Eventually, Bobby Horne began to find all this talk about space intelligences too oppressive and went back to his wife in Florida. Lyall Watson also declined to become a permanent part of the team, on the grounds that he had to get back to writing books. This left Puharich, Phyllis Schlemmer and Sir John Whitmore, whose fortune was to finance some of the hectic activity of the next two years.

The remainder of Holroyd's long book is too confusing to attempt a detailed summary. What happened, basically, was that Puharich, Whitmore and Phyllis Schlemmer spent a great deal of time rushing around the world – often suspected of being spies – and sitting in hotel rooms listening to instructions from "Tom" and praying for world peace. Periodically, "Tom" congratulated them and explained that they had just averted some international catastrophe, such as the assassination of the Palestinian leader, Yasser Arafat. The book ends, as all good books should, with a dramatic climax in which the three musketeers avert a Middle Eastern war by driving around Israel holding meditation sessions and otherwise "diffusing a vapor trail of love and peace." At the end of this agitated pilgrimage, "Tom" assures them that their efforts have been successful and that the Middle East will cease to be a flashpoint for some time to come. With a sound sense of literary structure, he even advises Puharich to use these events as the climax of the book he intends to write. (In fact, Puharich passed on the job to Stuart Holroyd.) We are told in a postscript that equally weird things have been taking place since the successful peace mission in March 1975, but that these must wait for a future instalment.

In the bibliography of *Prelude to the Landing on Planet Earth*, Holroyd cites a nineteenth-century classic of psychical investigation, *From India to the Planet Mars* by Theodore Flournoy, and readers of Holroyd may find the parallel instructive. In 1894, Flournoy, a well-known psychologist, investigated the mediumship of an attractive girl named Catherine Muller (whom he called Heléne Smith.) He was soon convinced of the genuineness

161

of her powers – she was able to tell him about events that occurred in his family before he was born. In later seances, Catherine went into deeper trances and began to describe her "past incarnations" – as the wife of a Hindu prince of the fifteenth century, as Marie Antoinette, and as an observer of life on Mars. Flournoy remains skeptical. The Hindu incarnation is often convincing: She seemed to have considerable knowledge of the language and customs of fifteenth-century India, and even named a prince, Sivrouka Nakaya, who was later found to have been a historical personage. By contrast, the descriptions of Mars are absurd, with yellow sky, red hills, bug-eyed monsters, and buildings that look just like human beings. Their language, as transcribed by her, is suspiciously like French.

If any charitable spiritualists felt inclined to give Catherine the benefit of the doubt, their justification for doing so vanished in September 1976, when the Viking landing on Mars revealed the planet to be an arid desert with no sign of life – even minute organisms.

Yet Catherine Muller cannot be dismissed as a fraud, even of the unconscious variety. Her knowledge of Flournoy's past showed that she possessed genuine powers of telepathy. While she was in trance, Flournoy witnessed "apports" of Chinese shells and coins, and even roses and violets in midwinter. Paranormal forces undoubtedly were at work but Flournoy declined to allow this to persuade him that Catherine had really been a Hindu princess or had visited Mars.

Flournoy would certainly have been equally skeptical about the narrative in *Prelude to a Landing on Planet Earth*. He would see no reason for rejecting the explanation that he applied to the mediumship of "Heléne Smith":

that the answers should be sought in the unconscious minds of the participants. And it must be admitted that Heléne's identification of herself with a Hindu princess and Marie Antoinette is, if anything, rather more believable that "Tom's" revelation that Puharich had once been the god Horus (and later, Pythagoras), while Whitmore had been Thoth and Phyllis Schlemmer, Isis . . . .

Still, in all fairness, one has to admit that anyone who experienced the events described in *The Sacred Mushroom, Uri* and *Prelude to the Landing on Planet Earth*, would end up convinced of the existence of space intelligences. If the whole thing is some kind of trick of the unconscious, how does it work? And *whose* unconscious?

One explanation could be that Puharich and Geller were both telepathic. Since Puharich was already convinced of the existence of the "Nine," it was logical – and almost inevitable – that Geller's trance messages should come from these non-human intelligences. In short, Geller and Puharich united to form a kind of firework display of poltergeist effects.

Naturally Puharich would not have agreed with this theory. He had long ago reached the conclusion that the "Nine" are a reality, and that our earth has been observed by spacemen for thousands of years. He believed that the earth has reached a point in its history where the "Nine" feel that slightly more intervention is necessary. But public miracles, like a mass landing of UFOs, are probably undesirable. Human beings have to evolve and learn to use their freedom. Too much "help" from outside would be disastrous because it would make us lazy and dependent, like some primitive tribe suddenly invaded by twentieth-century technology. Instead, Puharich believed, the extraterrestrials are concentrating on individuals, particularly children, so that the race is changed from within. He claimed he had studied a large number of children with astonishing psychic gifts, not simply the ability to bend spoons, but telepathy and other unusual powers. The great mathematical prodigies of the past, he thought, were a foreshadowing of what is to come.

The fact that so many of the "space intelligences" make contact through "mediums" suggests that we may be dealing with the same problem that arose in the mid-nineteenth century with the birth of "Spiritualism." In 1848, mysterious rappings in the house of the Fox family in Hydesville, New York, led to a nationwide interest in the subject of spirits. The rappings always took place in the presence of the two daughters of the family – aged 12 and 14 – and were probably some kind of poltergeist activity. But other "mediums" went into trances and were apparently able to communicate with the spirits of the dead. They were usually taken over by a "guide" who claimed to come from the "other world." The "Society for Psychical Research" was set up to investigate the phenomena scientifically, and eminent investigators – like Professor Earnest Bozzano, Professor Charles Richet, F. W. H. Myers – attempted to construct theories that would serve as a foundation for "psychic science." None of them came even remotely near to succeeding. Many mediums proved to be fraudulent, but so many were obviously genuine that the "Society for Psychical Research" soon became convinced that "the paranormal" *cannot* be dismissed as a delusion. In fact, some of their investigations were so successful that many came to believe that the final truth about the supernatural would be known by the end of the nineteenth century, and that ghosts would be as fully understood as electricity and magnetism.

Yet now, more than 100 years later, we know that such hopes were illusory. Psychical researchers still agree that most of the phenomena are *real*. But they are as far away as ever from an explanation. All of which points to the possibility that the same may prove to apply to the mystery of flying saucers.

Conclusions

UFO sightings continue to occur regularly all over the world. Whether or not you have not seen one yourself, someone you know almost certainly has. The frequency of sightings makes it impossible to dismiss them as something that simply does not happen.

The real question about UFOs is their origin – do they come from other planets or from within our own minds? Recent scientific discoveries seem to prove that it is almost certain that there are other life-forms in the universe.

Passengers at Akita airport, in northern Honshu, Japan, saw an unexpected object flying out of the sky on October 17, 1975. A local television reporter was the first to see the object hovering high over the runway. He immediately rang his office to file a report. In all, 50 people saw the object, which was described as a brilliant gold disc dotted with white lights. The captain of an airliner landing at the airport got a closer look. He described the object as resembling two dishes placed lip to lip, the classic UFO design. After five minutes of hovering, the disc set off westward out to sea.

Professor James T. Stanley (of the University of Washington), has found microbes that live happily inside Antarctic ice sheets. Other teams of researchers have found microbes in extremely hot and acidic conditions, for example, inside volcanoes.

Recent pictures taken by the Galileo space probe of Jupiter's moon, Europa, show that life could exist there. Europa's surface is made up of ice. Galileo's photographs show that the ice is made up of large sections, not unlike ice floes on earth. This, in turn, suggests that below the ice there is liquid water, probably kept unfrozen by volcanic activity. From what we know of life on earth, it seems possible that microbes could exist in such an environment. In fact, NASA itself has speculated that all the conditions for life seem likely to exist on Europa. If our own planetary system holds at least two potential sources of life, how many more must there be throughout the universe?

Of course, the existence of life on other planets does not in itself prove that UFOs are extraterrestrial spacecraft. Even if there is other life out there, it is a big assumption to say that it would have both the ability and the desire to visit earth. On the other hand, UFOs could be purely "psychic" phenomena, the latest expression of something that has been happening down the centuries.

No one who has studied psychic phenomena can fail to observe that they seem to *change* over long periods of time. Consider, for example, the strange history of the poltergeist, or "banging ghost." The earliest account we possess dates back to 858 AD in Germany, when an "evil spirit" threw stones and shook the walls of a farmhouse, "as though men were striking them with hammers."

166

There are several other accounts over the next few centuries, but one thing is clear – that such cases were rare. Chroniclers are anxious to mention them as proof of the existence of the spirit world, and therefore of Christianity. If there had been many such cases, we should have heard about them. Yet, in fact, anyone who looks into poltergeist phenomena will find that they are happening all the time. It would probably be accurate to say that there is a poltergeist case taking place within ten miles of where you are at present reading this book. In other words, their *number* has increased dramatically.

Again, ghosts and "spirits" were often recorded in earlier centuries. But in the mid-nineteenth century, when interest in "spiritualism" swept the world from America to Russia, there were suddenly thousands of cases. It was as if the "spirits" (or whatever they were), took advantage of this sudden interest in them to flood the world with their activities.

Perhaps the strangest case is that of the so-called vampire. Stories of vampires first reached the west in the early eighteenth century, when the Turks were driven out of eastern Europe. Doctors, priests and medical men reported cases in which dead people were seen walking the streets. When their graves were opened, their bodies were found undecayed as if newly buried. Dozens of reliable witnesses signed sworn statements describing the exhumation of these "living dead." In fact, vampire stories date back many centuries, but in earlier times they often sound like poltergeists, creating disturbances rather than attacking living people. It is very difficult to pin down the truth behind the tales of the vampire. All we know is that it has *changed* down the centuries.

And now, suddenly, it seems that we have a new form of "strange phenomenon," the UFO, complete with abductions and sinister men in black. Just as in the case of psychic phenomena, all efforts to understand it scientifically have run into a brick wall.

As long as UFOs keep being seen, there will be a wealth of theories to try to explain them. If they are alien craft, advances in communication and space travel may enable us to make contact with them. If they are psychic phenomena, they may be replaced by another embodiment of our troubled group mind. In either case, it seems likely that within 100 years, we will know the answer.

Index